Communicating the Future

For Oliver

Communicating the Future

Solutions for Environment, Economy, and Democracy

W. Lance Bennett

polity

First published in 2021 by Polity Press

Polity Press
65 Bridge Street
Cambridge CB2 1UR, UK

Polity Press
101 Station Landing
Suite 300
Medford, MA 02155, USA

ISBN-13: 978-1-5095-4044-0 (hardback)
ISBN-13: 978-1-5095-4045-7 (paperback)

A catalogue record for this book is available from the British Library.

Library of Congress Cataloging-in-Publication Data
Names: Bennett, W. Lance, author. | Polity Press.
Title: Communicating the future : solutions for environment, economy and democracy / W. Lance Bennett.
Description: Medford, Massachusetts : Polity Press, 2020. | Includes bibliographical references and index. | Summary: "A star scholar's treatise on how communication studies can lead to positive environmental change"-- Provided by publisher.
Identifiers: LCCN 2020022590 (print) | LCCN 2020022591 (ebook) | ISBN 9781509540440 (Hardback) | ISBN 9781509540457 (Paperback) | ISBN 9781509540464 (ePub) | ISBN 9781509545841 (Adobe PDF)
Subjects: LCSH: Communication in politics--United States. | Communication in the environmental sciences. | Mass media and the environment.
Classification: LCC JA85.2.U38 B46 2020 (print) | LCC JA85.2.U38 (ebook) | DDC 320.01/4--dc23
LC record available at https://lccn.loc.gov/2020022590
LC ebook record available at https://lccn.loc.gov/2020022591

Typeset in 10.5 on 12pt Sabon
by Fakenham Prepress Solutions, Fakenham, Norfolk NR21 8NL
Printed and bound in Great Britain by CPI Group (UK) Ltd, Croydon

For further information on Polity, visit our website:
www.politybooks.com

Contents

Acknowledgments

This book offers a framework for developing more effective political communication, based on principles of transparency and reason, to advance the greatest good for the greatest number of people and other species over the longest run. At the core of the argument is a model of how social movements, political leaders and citizens can develop and spread better ideas to replace environmentally destructive and socially unjust political and economic regimes. I hope this framework will be of interest to scholars, students, activists, and citizens.

Although the book is short in length, it reflects a long and wonderful journey in which I have been enlightened by many people. Many of the ideas here have been informed by exchanges with students and colleagues at the University of Washington, where, over the years, we created a number of learning communities to think about how better to align environment, economy, and democracy. An early project involved John de Graaf, Tim Jones, and dozens of students to explore the question: *What's the Economy For?* This is also the title of a book and film by John, who is one of my favorite renaissance people. Shortly after that, along came Deric Gruen, community activist and organizer extraordinaire, who helped me develop the Rethinking Prosperity project with students, community leaders, and progressive funders. Among other things, we learned a lot about how community organizations and funders can greatly improve (or unwittingly undermine) the capacity and sustainability of their programs for change.

Deric and I later teamed up with Alan Borning, a collaborator on past projects and a computer scientist, who is concerned about how his field can contribute more to the public good. We founded the SEED project (solutions for environment, economy, and democracy), which is also the subtitle of this book. SEED drew an interdisciplinary group of scholars and activists from different nations to discuss many of the issues raised in the following pages. I am indebted to everyone who shared this part of the journey, in particular, Alan, Deric, Volker Wulf, Markus Rohde, Hanna Hallin, Vicky Wenzelman, and a stimulating group of alternative economists who taught me a great deal. Thanks to Volker for the fun gatherings in Siegen. Alan, Deric, and Hanna also provided helpful comments on the manuscript. Paralleling the SEED project was a student-led learning community called the Sustainability Action Network from which I learned a lot about the challenges of bridging campus and community organizations scattered over different environmental, economic, and political causes. Thanks to the energetic students and to Scott Davis for his patience in helping to organize them.

Other colleagues at the University of Washington have contributed much to my thinking over the years, including: Matt Powers, Kirsten Foot, Mako Hill, Patricia Moy, Michael McCann, Chris Parker, Karen Litfin, Jamie Mayerfeld, and Jim Caporaso, among others. Adrienne Russell deserves a special acknowledgment for her perceptive and helpful reading of the manuscript. Special thanks to my department chairs John Wilkerson and Christine Harold, as well as the other administrators who have supported our work at the Center for Communication and Civic Engagement, and given me the flexibility to visit other universities and research institutes in developing this book.

The work of so many other colleagues has influenced my thinking about how transformative ideas spread that I cannot thank them all here. So, I want to express my appreciation for all of the excellent work in communication, political science, and my home field of political communication that has informed my thinking. However, there are a few people whose contributions call for special mention. Alexandra

Segerberg at Uppsala University always asks the best questions and spots the arguments that need fixing. Henrik Bang at Canberra challenged me to remember the importance of "everyday makers" like Greta Thunberg. Julie Uldam at Copenhagen Business School gave me some great feedback on the manuscript, and I share her hopes that more citizens and organizations working for change can overcome their "narcissism of small differences." And thanks to my good friend Brian Loader, who has spent many hours over scotch and conversation helping steer this project toward a balance of hope and realism within a useful analytical framework. Also, I appreciate being invited into the community of social movement scholars some years ago by Donatella della Porta and Sidney Tarrow. Insights from many members of that network have found their way into this book.

The plan of the book began to emerge during time spent with colleagues at various universities and research centers in Europe. I am grateful to Barbara Pfetsch, who nominated me for a Humboldt Research Award, and to the Alexander von Humboldt Foundation for granting me recurring visits to Free University, Berlin, between 2015 and 2017, where I developed early sketches of the project. Spending the fall of 2018 and winter 2019 as a research fellow at the Weizenbaum Institute for the Networked Society (The German Internet Institute) in Berlin helped my thinking about how disinformation of the kind surrounding our environment debates is produced and how it travels over media networks. I am grateful to Barbara Pfetsch and her teams at Weizenbaum for the many lively discussions, with particular thanks to Curd Knüpfer, Ulrike Klinger, and Annette Heft, among others. My time in Berlin was also enriched by discussions with Peter Lohauss on green economics (and rock and roll), Maria Haberer on democracy and progressive activism, and Terry Martin for his wit and wisdom in commenting on early drafts and much else.

Serious writing on the book began in the spring of 2019 during a research fellowship at the Institute for Advanced Sustainability Studies in Potsdam. Thanks to Henrike Knappe and Patrizia Nanz for making this possible. Achim Mass and the team who ran the fellowship program at IASS made my stay incredibly rich. I am particularly grateful for the weekly seminars featuring fellows from all over the world presenting research on an incredible range of environmental problems, including their social and economic aspects. I was humbled by the wisdom and generosity of both the fellows and IASS researchers. Ortwin Renn was particularly helpful for my thinking about bridging questions of science and society. I also want to thank Frank Fischer for his refreshing perspectives on public policy processes, and Frank and Dorota Stasiak for their collaboration in organizing a workshop on climate science disinformation. The IASS staff made it all go smoothly. And special thanks to Danniel Gobbi who participated in the workshop, and shared original material on the connection between Charles Koch political operations in the US and the movements that helped elect Jair Bolsonaro in Brazil.

The opportunity to help organize and join a Social Science Research Council working group during 2018 to 2020 on the history of media technology and disinformation taught me a lot about *The Disinformation Age*, which is the title of the book produced by that group. In particular, I have enjoyed my conversations with Steven Livingston, who helped me clarify the rise of neoliberal economics and associated democratic disruptions discussed in Chapter 3.

To Mary Savigar, my wonderful editor at Polity, I can only say that without you, this book might not exist at all, and surely not in its current form. Mary helped me develop the project, sort out the many ways to write it, and offered the perfect guidance in finding the right tone and approach. Ellen MacDonald-Kramer kept me on track through the process. Thanks also for the excellent suggestions from the two anonymous reviewers.

Finally, I thank my life partner and intellectual companion Sabine Lang for the careful reading and helpful ideas on the final draft of the manuscript. Her insights are informed by knowing what I am trying to write, sometimes even better than I do. Sabine has the rare ability to find, and suggest how to fix, all the places that make an argument stronger.

As I write these words, the world is in the grip of a coronavirus pandemic (named Covid-19 for Coronavirus disease of 2019). It has been challenging to think about the future when the human toll is so immediate, and the economic crisis looms so large. It is ironic that as economies around the world shut down, demand for oil collapsed and industrial pollution eased; many environmental health indicators improved. This book is an expression of hope that we can find ways to organize our economic and political lives in better balance with the life support capacities of the planet. The world seems both far away and terrifyingly close from our small retreat on a peninsula less than two hours from the complexities of Seattle. It is inspiring to be surrounded by islands, trees, mountains, and water. It seems a good omen that a pair of eagles flew by as I wrote these last words.

Longbranch, Washington, May 2020

Introduction: The Future is Now

Thinking about the environment and the future of life on the planet is challenging. The daily news is filled with stories about serious threats on so many fronts. At the same time, there is hope in the uprisings of millions of people, all over the world, who demand political action. A surprising leader of millions of young people who protested around the globe was a sixteen-year-old Swedish girl named Greta Thunberg, who left school to hold a one-person strike for climate change outside the Parliament building in Stockholm in 2018. Her eloquence and ability to focus attention on children concerned about their futures soon won her invitations to speak at the United Nations. She is the girl who took a 32-hour train ride from Sweden to the Alps to address The World Economic Forum, and scolded the world elite for flying in on their private jets. Her courage and eloquence won her a Nobel Peace Prize nomination in 2019. In a speech before the British Parliament, she said this:

> My name is Greta Thunberg. I am 16 years old. I come from Sweden. And I speak on behalf of future generations…
>
> I was fortunate to be born in a time and place where everyone told us to dream big … People like me had everything we could ever wish for and yet now we may have nothing…

> Now we probably don't even have a future any more. Because that future was sold so that a small number of people could make unimaginable amounts of money. It was stolen from us every time you said that the sky was the limit, and that you only live once.[1]

Students around the world began walking out of school and taking to the streets in a movement they named "Fridays for Future." Anna Taylor, aged seventeen, helped found the UK student climate network and was soon making eloquent statements of her own to the national press: "Those in power are not only betraying us and taking away our future, but are responsible for the climate crisis that's unfolding in horrendous ways around the world." Pointing out that climate change affects those least responsible for the causes, and least able to do anything about it, she also noted that, "It is our duty to not only act for those in the UK and our futures, but for everyone. That's what climate justice means."[2]

For those who believe the overwhelming scientific evidence, an ecological crisis threatens the current human civilization built on fossil fuels, overconsumption of resources, negligent handling of wastes, and a built-for-obsolescence consumer culture. Many animal species beyond humans are threatened as well. We hear most often about global warming, but there are many other earth system breakdowns caused by the runaway industrialization of nature. Frightening cocktails of toxics are found routinely in air, water, soil, and food. Interactions among different environmental hazards multiply present dangers and bring new ones. Precious water supplies are increasingly contaminated by agricultural chemicals, landfill leakage, industrial and human wastes, hydraulic fracking for natural gas and oil, and dozens of other sources. Supplies of clean water in some regions are further compromised by glacial melting due to global heating. The liquidation of vast ice sheets at the poles and Greenland is causing rising sea levels that threaten massive population migrations from coastal areas. Loss of arable land due to draught, deforestation, and soil deterioration threatens famine and even greater human migrations. There is a sixth great species extinction under way, with cascading effects on food supplies, pest populations, and health. Add

X-factors such as the Covid-19 pandemic to this precarious mix, and it begins to be clear how fragile this planetary house of cards has become. For many inhabitants of economically prosperous regions, these multiplying catastrophes once seemed distant and abstract, but now they are hitting closer to home.

There is much magical thinking that technologies such as renewable energy or electric cars will save us, but there is little evidence that they can make enough difference to turn the tide. The hopes placed in Green technologies are understandable, but most of them have hidden resource costs and limited potential to support continued economic growth on a global scale. One way or another, we are near the end of a centuries-long economic binge that has witnessed the harvest and waste of resources well beyond anything that can be renewed and absorbed by planetary capacities. Even before the global economic shock of Covid-19, we were approaching a great moment of truth and choice between staying on the same catastrophic economic path or transitioning to more livable outcomes for people and other species in regions facing different local versions of the crisis.

Rather than hide from the future and suffer the worst-case disasters, perhaps we can imagine futures based on values such as: rebuilding communities, making products with more lasting value, reducing unproductive financial speculation, rewarding socially productive – if less profitable – investment in education, health, and other public services, and creating work that provides decent lives. This will require adjusting obscene inequalities in wealth so that the rich and powerful live closer to the realities inhabited by the rest of us and come to see that we share a common fate. Achieving this best-case scenario requires developing and communicating positive visions of change that motivate political realignment behind a new economics. This is no easy task, but it is possible with a more unified politics and the communication strategies to spread ideas and promote policies.

Millions of protesters around the world have drawn public and political attention to the planetary extinction crisis. After making the environment a more pressing concern, the important political question at this point is: What do we do now? That question is the focus of this book. The answers offered here involve changing how we think, communicate, organize, and act. It may be surprising to learn that this is not as difficult as it sounds, because this is an argument for bringing our communication processes and politics more in line with the nature of the problems we face.

The path to more effective political action involves communicating about economics, politics, and environment, together, in ways that offer more appealing images of change than commonly associated with proposals for carbon taxes or radical sacrifices in how we consume and live. Various personal adjustments will surely come at some point down the road, but this is the wrong end of the problem to emphasize now. Many people are already living at the margins, both north and south, and there is little to gain from making the road ahead seem even worse. Broad public support for positive change is needed to pressurize political parties in democracies for better policies that package equity and environment together.

Finding ways to develop and spread ideas that might actually make a difference is challenging for many reasons, including: resistance from short sighted business interests; caution from parties and governments captured by those interests; and disinformation from growing rightwing movements that have mobilized large publics against many progressive policies, including climate change. Rightwing organizations in Europe and the US even found a German teenager named Naomi Seibt to play the role of the "anti-Greta" on YouTube, in publications, and at conferences in the US and Europe.

It is easy to blame the lack of decisive progress on the environmental crisis on business interests, timid politicians, the noise from popular movements, and leaders on the radical right. While those factors loom large, it is also time to put the spotlight on the millions of concerned citizens, environmental organizations, and aligned activists who have done an excellent job sounding alarms and winning small victories but continue to lose the larger fight for a more livable future. Those calling for change are majorities in many nations. It is time for us all to change our thinking about the role of communication in building stronger political action networks that can develop and spread clearer ideas about more livable societies. And we need to understand how transformative ideas acquire the clarity and commitment to fuel movements that resonate with publics and politicians.

At the core of the problem is how we routinely communicate about complex problems like climate change and the many other symptoms of environmental collapse that intersect with critical life spheres such as economics and politics. The language and logics that we encounter in news accounts, from experts and politicians, and in everyday conversations, tend to chop big problems up into small solutions that don't add up. And even those approaches often employ backwards thinking that focuses on treating symptoms rather than underlying causes. It turns out that many communication scholars and practitioners also approach complex problems with relatively narrow communication models based on message framing, audience targeting, or trying to set political and media agendas. Even when these strategies are successful, the resulting proposals mainly address environmental symptoms such as reducing carbon emissions, rather than focusing on underlying economic causes of continuing rising economic demand for fossil fuels. Better communication entails recognizing that complex problems typically have intersecting causes: for example, environmental problems are fundamentally economic and political in nature. The challenge is to develop simple models that enable better communication about this.

Rather than continue to reproduce communication that does not work well, we now have the capacity to understand and shape how transformational ideas flow in societies. We can explain a good deal about dense flows of content that involve rich mixes of images, memes, political slogans, scientific evidence, narratives, and the media influencers who bridge, filter, or block idea flows across different networks. We can use these understandings to help civil-society organizations, movements, concerned citizens, and politicians better coordinate the production, packaging, and networking of game-changing ideas. Communication scholars can find new ways to assemble old concepts, and add a few new ones, with the aim of better understanding how networked communication processes engage and organize people in complex media ecologies.

In short, the challenge for positive political change is not so much what to do about the radical right; in most democracies they are greatly outnumbered by citizens concerned about the environment and economic failures. Even business resistance is beginning to soften in some sectors, and investors are finally figuring out that oil stocks may not have such a bright future. The challenge ahead is for environmental, new economy, and political reform organizations (and their funders!) to develop more coherent ideas that offer positive visions for a more sustainable future. Unified movements spreading those ideas can engage voters and help leverage political parties to take action. If these things happen, then attractive packages such as The Green New Deal will be filled with truly transformative ideas.

Communicating the Future is not a book that invents new proposals for building a better world. There are plenty of good ideas about economic and democratic reform already in circulation, many dating back more than half a century. If simply writing about good ideas caused social and political change, we would not be in the current mess. The main focus of the book is on what has been missing: a simple model that citizens, organizations, and communication scholars can use to think and act differently about a set of problems that current approaches are failing to solve. This model of how ideas flow in society shows how think tanks, activist organizations, funders, and engaged publics can: (a) develop communication processes that (b) better enable diverse groups in different societies (c) to build stronger networks with common agendas, (d) that gain support in elections and policy processes, and (e) receive uptake from political parties and governments. Until these things happen, the reactionary right will continue to outperform the radical left in elections, and parties on the center left (e.g. European Social Democrats, US Democrats) and the center right (e.g. Christian Democrats) will continue to drift.

To aid the reader's thinking about building more effective models of political communication, the book shows how other transformative ideas have traveled in society and into politics. For example, Chapter 3 traces the origins and spread of the core principles of the currently dystopian economic system of global, deregulated, and ecologically predatory capitalism. The current economic operating systems in most nations will continue to defeat efforts to treat the multiplying environmental symptoms until coalitions of different stakeholders develop and implement more attractive alternatives. The aim is to show how those already concerned about the future can develop ideas about more equitable and ecologically sound societies and organize more effective politics to guide the transitions.

A place to start is with assessing the ever-expanding lists of specific issues that do not add up to a compelling vision for change: save the polar bears, stop oil drilling in the Arctic, protect the old growth forests, quit mining coal, stop burning the Amazon, tax carbon, build more renewable energy, and on and on. As our failing economic and political practices create more and more problems, it is easy to understand why so much energy is focused on trying to deal with them all. However, as noted earlier, the politics attached to all of that issue-specific communication generally ends up fighting the symptoms of an economic system that spews more new problems than any amount of issue-by-issue action can fix. Moreover, all of those worthy causes compete against each other for attention, empathy and action.

The logic of issue fragmentation in much of our political communication is, of course, reinforced in most democracies by governmental policy processes that compartmentalize issues in different legislative and bureaucratic sectors. Many of us live in democracies shaped after World War II, with institutions built on assumptions that socioeconomic systems were working fairly well, and that policy processes should address relatively narrow categories of things that required adjustments. As a result, civil-society organizations with lobbying capacities are pushed to develop political strategies to fit their issues into available political slots, and, above all, to "be realistic" in order to get a seat at the bargaining table. But so far, being realistic has not produced success beyond occasionally making the problems less bad. The legacy of "being realistic" has resulted in the reality that nineteen of the twenty hottest years ever recorded occurred in the first two decades of this century. Much of this heat is absorbed by the oceans, where water temperatures are also the highest in recorded history. There is a great species extinction currently in progress. And, despite gains in renewable energy, the global demand for fossil fuels continues to grow, driven by government subsidies in many nations for the coal, oil, and gas extraction needed to run economies that cannot function on renewables as currently configured. In 2019, Oxford dictionaries declared "climate emergency" the word of the year. Perhaps a better framing for the problem would be "economic emergency."

The political fragmentation that undermines movement coherence is also reinforced by the funders of cause organizations. Most funding programs encourage activities centered around specific issues, from saving birds and other endangered species, to figuring out how to grow food in increasingly marginal environments. Private and public funders that support civil-society organizations must find ways to introduce broader connectivity among their funding networks and provide incentives for organizations to cooperate in developing more broadly shared visions.

In short, it is time to rethink movement politics so that diverse factions can share common economic critique and renewal strategies, and march under fewer banners. It is good to remember that alarms about the relentless industrialization and degradation of nature have been sounded continuously by growing numbers of movement organizations, citizens, and scientists since at least the middle of the last century. Over the decades, the modern environmental movement, though loosely organized, has grown into the largest continuing expression of citizen concern and outrage on the planet. This book addresses the challenge of what to do after sounding the alarm. It is important to understand both how communication has contributed to the current crisis, and that we can learn to develop and share more effective ideas about more sustainable economies and societies.

Beyond the millions of schoolchildren and "extinction rebels" focusing public attention on the future, there are promising signs of public readiness to act. For example, opinion trends in the US show solid majorities favoring more effective environmental action even if it slows economic growth.[3] But where are the appealing ideas, or the cohesive movements and voter publics that share those visions? And how can emerging political idea networks include more politicians, parties, and governments able to lead positive transitions toward better futures?

Despite many decades of activism and rising public concern, there are few widely shared visions of how people in different places can live well without destroying nature. To be clear: there are good and impressively documented ideas about how we can live differently and happily, but they have not yet become the focus of communication from large networks of prominent organizations working for change. Instead, we hear calls to stop eating meat, curb consumerism, or curtail travel. While such changes might help, many of the practices they attack are deeply embedded in many societies and cannot just be pulled out of the middle of people's lives. Until such proposals are supported by more comprehensive plans that contain motivating visions of better ways of living, they will not gain the political uptake required to make a difference. As a result, the burden of change is often left up to individuals, who cannot organize change on the scale that is required.

A place to start is with learning how to develop, share, and amplify ideas that offer alternatives to currently dominant practices and their rationalizations. For example, there are many fragmentary movements and organizations producing sound alternatives to dominant thinking about the necessity of economic growth promoted with little consideration about what kinds of growth with what kinds of social benefits. The common prayer for economic growth has become the secular religion of our time. Yet the idea of engineering economic growth is a relatively recent historical invention that emerged, with theories and methods attached, in the wake of the Great Depression of the 1930s. Earlier economic thinking regarded growth as an incidental byproduct of more fundamental economic relations and outcomes. Nevertheless, the growth hype quickly promised a singular vision of prosperity that was conveniently blind to the costs, both human and environmental, that became built into our everyday cultures.

And so, we live with a daily backdrop of media cheerleading for growth, pronouncements from economists who serve as the high priests of our secular economic religion, and daily consumer propaganda to buy more stuff. Sadly, this is a false religion. Kenneth Boulding, a prominent economist and environment advisor to US President Kennedy in the 1960s, once quipped: "Anyone who believes in indefinite growth in anything physical, on a physically finite planet, is either mad or an economist."[4] More recently, economist James K. Galbraith has observed that: "Postwar neoclassical growth theories deliberately ignored resource and environmental limits, disparaged and disdained ecologists, and promised what was effectively impossible: perpetual growth, fueled by unlimited resources, the free disposal of wastes, and never-ending technological progress. Early warnings ... [about environmental limits] ... were ridiculed. More recently, the science of limits has gained acceptance, but most economists remain preoccupied with growth."[5] It is ironic that the basis for spreading the gospel of growth in the last century has evaporated in economies racked by inequality, austerity, and debt. While it was once fashionable to think that a rising economic tide lifts all boats, Galbraith quipped that, today, "a rising tide lifts only yachts."[6]

The good news is that opportunities for change are present. The world economy was already struggling on artificial life support (i.e. debt-driven growth) before the Covid-19 pandemic. The resulting shutdown of national economies produced shocks that invited a return to greater government management of economies based on concerns about public welfare. But what should governments do? There is even good news on this front: many creative ideas already exist for how to build "circular" or "steady state" economies, as discussed later in the book. These ideas aim to bring systems of production, distribution, consumption, and waste management into better balance with life-support systems on the planet. The time is ripe to fashion a new set of life stories from these ideas. In order to make a difference, a broad spectrum of organizations must develop the capacity to design, package, and promote more common visions of economic and political change.

Even though the opportunities for political renewal are growing, political parties have been slow to take advantage of them – at their own peril. Polls and election results in nations such as the UK, the US, Australia, and Germany indicate that the messages of the traditionally dominant parties (e.g. European Christian Democrats and Social Democrats, UK Labour, US Republicans and Democrats) have become exhausted following their neoliberal turns of the 1980s and 1990s and the related loss of their traditional voter bases. While there has been a resurgence of Green parties in Europe, some Green factions continue to put politics over principle by forming coalitions with center-right partners that limit their capacity for economic reforms. The idea of "Green growth" has become a fig leaf for abandoning transformative economics in a time of environmental crisis. More broadly, few center-left parties have figured out how to engage former working classes that have been replaced by a growing "precariat" of underemployed service and gig workers, who have yet to find (or to be offered) a political identity.[7] A renewal of political parties with more credible appeals to discouraged publics can set a better political course.

Until better coordinated political networks engage publics to spread common ideas about positive change, those visions will be overshadowed by the daily propaganda from business, politicians, and economists who fill the news with economic ideas that turn out to be life threatening. Unless activists, politicians, businesses, political parties, and publics can imagine more sustainable economic models, far less attractive outcomes are likely to result from crisis and disruption. The Covid-19 pandemic revealed both the fragility of global economies, and importance of governments in managing chaos. Instead of waiting for both economy and environment to pull each other down, it seems prudent to offer receptive leaders and parties ideas and policy packages that match the scale and pace of the crisis.

With these political considerations in mind, the core questions guiding this book are: *How to better coordinate, define, and scale up the communication of more effective economic and political ideas?* and *How to create the popular understanding and demand for political uptake required to give those ideas a political chance?* Democracies that still merit the name must begin experimenting with other ways to make economies work. And, if they want to be more relevant and effective, mainstream environmental organizations would do well to embrace ideas about economic change. Unless citizens and activists communicate a more widely shared economic vision, it will be difficult to pressure political leaders and parties to embrace policies that will actually make a difference. These communication shifts do not need to occur just on the left. There are also signs that many people on the center right of the political spectrum are open to thinking about environmental economics centered around themes of localism, energy security, support for small businesses, and promoting elements of the good life, such as leisure, family, community, less pollution, better transportation, and improved health.[8] The point is that that it is possible to ease partisan divides by challenging the prevailing mindset that economy and environment are competing entities, and instead show that they are best understood as inseparable.

Communicating the Future offers a framework that citizens, advocates, and communication scholars can use to approach complex human problems like the environmental crisis in new ways. Communication has been instrumental in getting us into the current mess, and it can also help us set a different course. Communication for change involves developing techniques to: (a) evaluate common but unproductive communication that blocks thinking about change, (b) develop ideas and narratives that intersect the categories of economic, political, and environmental problems, and (c) design communication processes that help organize and engage diverse publics to demand more effective solutions.

A first step in this journey is to realize that communicating effectively about the future is really about how we communicate about economics and politics now. As many of those sounding the alarms have pointed out, the crisis is already here. Bill McKibben put it well in the title of a commentary called: "Don't Imagine the Future – It's Already Here."[9] What this means is that the real problems are embedded in the social, political, and economic institutions that structure our daily lives today. Meaningful change starts with learning to dislodge the categorical thinking that limits the collective imagination. For example, environmental questions might better be framed like this: Assume that we want to protect life quality on the planet, what kinds of economics do we need to adopt, and what do we need to modify? In other words, there is much to gain by translating environmental questions into economic ones. In addition to pointing to more direct solutions for problems, this shift in framing environmental issues has advantages in institutional politics where economic considerations generally take top priority.

Until environmental advocates, funding organizations, citizens, and politicians develop appealing economic visions and the networked organization to spread them, they will continue to lose environmental policy fights to those who simply raise economic anxieties. Learning to communicate at the intersection of environment, economy, and politics entails recognizing that communication is more than just framing and exchanging messages to promote specific issues or campaigns. Communication is most powerful when ideas are produced and packaged so that they can travel over different social networks and flow into popular narratives about who we are and how we want to live.

Overview of the Book

Communicating the Future is based on the idea that communication is more than just sending and receiving messages. Ideas, and how we develop and spread them, constitute the social, economic, and political networks that are integral to how we organize and change our lives. This book explores how these communication processes work, and how citizens and organizations can communicate differently to replace current economic and political practices based on ideas that function poorly for people and planet. This does not mean that positive change can occur overnight, but there is hope in using communication to develop and guide manageable transitions away from the economics and politics that currently threaten life on the planet. This book also shows how the dysfunctional economic ideas that still dominate our lives gained such dominance, and how we can think and act differently about the future.

Chapter 1 presents a set of basic communication concepts and exercises that help decode frequently encountered, but unhelpful, arguments about environment, economy, and politics that circulate through legacy and social media. Following these warmup exercises, Chapter 1 introduces a model of how ideas that make an impact tend to travel or flow in society. This *idea-flow model* introduces transformative communication in society as a process that involves: (1) coordinated development and *production* of ideas, with illustrations ranging from crowd production to more industrial models utilizing think tanks, strategic communication campaigns, and political organizations, (2) effective *packaging* of ideas using creative categorization, framing, narration, emotional cuing, and easy breakdown into memes and story elements that travel over different networks, (3) strategies for better *network alignment* for sharing ideas among diverse stakeholders such as business interests, civil-society organizations, publics, and parties, resulting in (4) unified movements positioning ideas for *political uptake* by pressurizing political leaders and parties when opportunities arise.

Chapter 2 uses the *idea-flow model* to show how to organize and share better integrated economic and environmental visions with the potential for broad political uptake. This entails recognizing the important ideas that have come from the environmental movement. At the same time, it is important to see how the movement has become spread out around different causes and different arenas of issue politics. The discussion provides keys for using communication as an organizational process to better align the environmental movement both internally, and with a broader spectrum of economic justice and political reform organizations to build a more effective politics for change. The task is made somewhat easier by the richness of many ideas already in circulation that just need more amplification and coordinated promotion.

Chapter 3 shows how the idea-flow model was used effectively by the so-called neoliberal economics movement that gained broad political uptake toward the end of the last century. The reorganization of politics around ideas of limited government, restricted popular control over economies, privatization of many public services, and the deregulation of many business sectors, has subordinated modern environmentalism to a set of unfortunate political tradeoffs in which jobs and economic growth generally compromise stronger ecological economic policies. By many measures, the neoliberal brand of political economy has run its course, not least in terms of growing inequality, the rising environmental costs of doing business, and the perversion of its own ideals due to oligarchy and crony capitalism. Yet this idea regime remains widely in power, and increasingly antagonistic to liberal democracy. The question is how more attractive alternatives can become better positioned for political uptake. The idea-flow model allows us to compare the differences between the rise of this elite-driven neoliberal political economy movement, and the prospects for greater coordination of communication and ideas among environmentalists, economic justice advocates, and democratic reform groups. Even if we accept the idea that more effective communication involves communicating at the intersection of political, economic, and environmental ideas, we also must learn to package those ideas to improve flow across diverse networks, including politicians, parties, and business elites, which can help with the uptake of new economic ideas into higher circles of politics and power.

Chapter 4 examines the current resistance to fundamental economic change among many business and political elites. In those circles, what is "realistic," often means making environmental adjustments only at the margins, or talking about Green growth, without changing the basic economic practices that endanger a livable future. The irony is that environmental changes are already disrupting economies in many places, and are likely to make current production, work and consumption arrangements even more chaotic and less manageable. When such disruptions occur, they can be understood as political opportunities for change. Throughout modern history, social movements have helped spread new ideas in society and fueled passions for change. Among the reasons for hope today are the tens of thousands of civil-society organizations and millions of people already working for economic, environmental, or political change. As noted earlier, organizations promoting various causes are currently scattered across arbitrarily separated categories of action, and over an expanding array of problems. Developing the capacity to organize more aligned communication and action networks can change that.

Just what are the inspiring ideas around which more effective challenges can be based? Who will produce them? How can communication networks be strengthened across current issue and cause boundaries? Those are the questions addressed in Chapter 5. As noted in the Introduction, the good news is that there are already many well-developed ideas about ways to change our thinking about growth, investment, production, consumption, food supplies, wastes, and other basic aspects of living. So, the real goal is not to produce radical new ideas, but to design communication processes aimed at better developing and sharing existing models for change. This means improving the political alignment among diverse movement organizations, funders, research institutes, and think tanks. Organizations do not need to give up their primary missions. Rather, those missions can be enhanced by featuring values and goals already held in common: economic fairness, strong communities, social wellbeing, businesses that offer more value to workers, communities, and environment; addressing inequalities within and between nations; enabling different models of development in poorer nations; better management of resources and wastes by business and government; and better connecting political parties and publics who care about these things. The time is ripe for better produced, packaged, and networked ideas at the intersection of economy, environment, and political renewal, combined with pressure for uptake by political parties and leadership. *Communicating the Future* shows how creative communication can get us there.

1
Communicating Complex Problems

When the world economy melted down following the Great Recession of the early twenty-first century, many governments declared the banks that were responsible for the crisis too big to fail. The resulting bailouts at taxpayer expense fueled a spiral of public sector and wage austerity that continues to this day. One may debate the wisdom of the methods used to stave off economic collapse, but one thing seems clear: much the same economy that produced the crisis – and that is driving the environment to extinction – was restored. There were few changes to the operating logic of risky, debt driven, and speculative growth. Nor were many changes made to tax and investment policies that send profits up the corporate and investment food chains, and push risk and inequality down to taxpayers and workers. Most leaders and experts spoke of restoring economic growth through much the same economic activities as before.

The folly of restoring the existing economic system was magnified by the Covid-19 pandemic that came along just as many national economies were beginning to recover from the Great Recession. One glaring warning sign was that at the peak of the health crisis in 2020, with factories, offices, travel, oil production, and many other normal operations cut back, CO_2 emissions were reduced by 5.5 percent in the first quarter, and projected at around 8 percent by the end of

2020 by the International Energy Agency.[1] Even though that represented the largest drop in emissions ever recorded, it roughly corresponded to the estimates of 7.6 percent reductions each year from 2020 to 2030 deemed necessary by scientists in the Intergovernmental Panel on Climate Change (IPCC) to hold rising temperatures below the danger line of 1.5 degrees Celsius. Beyond that red line, life conditions for life on the planet are expected to move from dangerous to catastrophic.[2] The implication is that the existing global economy must stall in order to meet minimum requirements for ecological survival. And yet, similar to the bailouts following the financial crisis, many governments propped up airlines, oil companies, and other polluting businesses deemed necessary to continue "normal" economic activities. Unless thinking about environment and economy become integrated in ways that enable imagining a 'new normal' that supports more resilient societies, the second great opportunity of this century will also be lost.[3]

To apply the economic logic of the financial crisis or the Covid-19 pandemic to the environment, it is hard to imagine what an environmental "bailout" might even look like – beyond the literal image of trying to turn back rising waters by any means necessary. Instead of policies that might work, we hear soothing phrases, from the evergreen idea of *sustainable development* to more recent political incantations for *Green growth*. These empty promises amount to magical thinking, involving a simple trick of categorical reasoning: we take an attractive feature of category A (the popular belief that growth is good), and combine it with an attractive element from category B (Green policies are good), mix with appealing language from politicians, and we have a reassuring idea that sounds much better than it works.

Because many citizens have come to doubt such empty political promises, environmental activism has continued at high levels. However, as noted in the introduction, it is easier to sound alarms than to develop broad programs of action that are likely to work. The scale of environmental emergencies makes it easy to see why so much energy is spent sounding alarms. During the summer before Covid-19 stole the headlines, the news reported that vast sections of Alaska, Siberia, Greenland, and other areas inside the Arctic

Circle were ablaze. The World Meteorological Organization estimated that the carbon dioxide produced by the fires in just one month equaled the total annual emissions of Sweden. At the same time, something called a "heat dome" settled over Greenland, creating a feedback cycle causing historic levels of ice melt. The same heat system was parked earlier over Europe, breaking temperature records, as Paris soared to 108 degrees Fahrenheit, helping to make July of 2019 the hottest month ever recorded on the planet.

As the earth continued its orbit around the sun, fires and record heat swept Australia. In addition to killing an estimated billion animals and creating some of the worst air pollution on the planet, the fires produced more carbon dioxide than the annual emissions of more than one hundred nations. In something of a theater of the absurd, Prime Minister Scott Morrison, an inveterate climate-change denier, ordered the Sydney fireworks to go ahead to show the world how optimistic the people were, even though fires and smoke had choked the city much of the summer. Undaunted by reality, Australian tourism authorities launched a campaign to lure post-Brexit tourists from the UK to the beaches of Oz. The ads featured Kylie Minogue singing, dancing, and lounging on pristine beaches, even as real Australian beaches were surrounded by fires that trapped thousands of actual tourists.

The language of denial is often as impenetrable as the atmosphere in the regions on fire. In that same fateful summer, more than 70,000 fires burned in the Amazon forests, many of them started to clear land for farming cattle and soybeans. The smoke turned daytime into night as far away as São Paulo, some 1,700 miles to the south. Earlier in the century, Brazil had improved its stewardship of the rainforest, but the election of a radical right government reversed those trends. The new Brazilian President, Jair Bolsonaro blocked conservation activities, suppressed record keeping by government agencies, and cut funds to environmental nongovernmental organizations (NGOs). He then blamed the fires on revenge from the NGOs and topped it off by accusing actor and environmentalist Leonardo DiCaprio of donating money to the organizations that set the fires. Fighting the facts of environmental collapse with conspiracy and disinformation continued as the Brazilian foreign minister declared climate change a Marxist plot. That claim followed the lead of US President Trump, who had long before declared climate change a Chinese hoax.

Beyond the smoke screens of enabling politicians are the realities of too much oil continuing to be burned and hundreds of new coal plants under construction around the world. Prominent energy companies have long covered up the dangers of their products. For example, leaked documents reveal that Shell and Exxon conducted research in the 1980s showing that their products were speeding climate change. Yet those reports were buried in order not to disturb investors and governments. Instead of pursuing other business models, the largest of the energy companies doubled down. They helped fund think tanks to produce disinformation and denials that such changes were occurring. And they have lobbied for more drilling in Arctic regions now accessible due to melting ice.

The locked-in commitments to oil are revealed in business networks that favor profits above all. The leadership of JP Morgan Bank asked Lee Raymond to continue on its board, despite major shareholder concerns that when Raymond was CEO of Exxon and later Exxon Mobil, he presided over the cover-up of known product harms and authorized funding of think tanks and other organizations running major disinformation campaigns. The bank clearly signaled its desire to continue on the path that generated a fortune by being the world's largest lender to fossil fuel companies.

Although pressure from activists and pension-fund shareholders produced a commitment to stop investing in Arctic drilling operations, JP Morgan continued to send mixed signals by criticizing the Green New Deal efforts in the US, while joining a climate action investor coalition and issuing PR statements about its support for renewables. Meanwhile, in Europe, the big energy companies have fought to make sure that the hard-won victories of environmentalists such as the Paris Climate Agreement would fall far short of stabilizing the ominous trends. Exxon Mobil, BP, and Shell spent over $100 million during the decade of 2010–2020 lobbying the European Union to water down its climate policies, including schemes to slow the conversion to electric vehicles in the European Green Deal.[4] All of this is about protecting the massive fossil fuel reserves already owned and identified by companies in the coal, gas, and oil business. The profits of those companies depend on being able to continue harvesting, selling, and burning those reserves. According to their stock reports, big energy companies have more than five times the fossil fuel reserves allowed by models simulating extreme climate disaster scenarios. As Bill McKibben put it: "The fossil fuel industry has five times the carbon needed to break the planet, and they're clearly planning to burn it."[5] Unless we begin thinking in terms that integrate economics, environment, and politics, and develop a new economic normal we will never end the underlying demand that is burning and poisoning the planet.

The dirty secret here is that as long as our current economic operating systems remain unchallenged, the ongoing demand for fossil fuels will crash the environment, and, eventually, the economy into the bargain. Unless civil-society organizations, funders, and political parties begin to coordinate and spread economic ideas with greater popular appeal, political struggles for the future will continue to occur around the margins of current economic systems. And even those fights will pit small environmental groups against more powerful industrial giants.

Until compelling alternative visions are positioned for political uptake, the default option is to continue living with economies deemed by elites as too big to fail, or even change very much. And we will live with the rantings of the Trumps, Bolsonaros, and Modis of the future, along with continuing deception from big energy companies and the economic interests that depend on them. Instead of using the oil crash associated with the Covid-19 crisis to shift public investments to renewable energy, the Trump administration pressed to support oil companies. Rather than use such opportunities to move in new directions, the default option among many elites is to continue propping up shaky economies that grow farther out of balance with the life-support systems of the planet. Deadly economic byproducts, from resource depletion, to CO_2 pollution, and a long list of toxic wastes, all continue to increase, despite the reassuring talk that many economies are getting Greener.

The intent here is not to raise fear levels in the reader (unless it is fear of current political communication logics). Scary visions are not helpful for thinking about how to better match the economy with the environment. I am reminded of a TV interview with David Wallace-Wells, author of a provocative book titled *The Uninhabitable Earth*. After the author listed some of the catastrophes likely to befall us – cities under water, massive population migrations with no place to go, health crises, and economic collapse – the interviewer looked plaintively at him and said, "Let's end on some hope."[6]

One hopeful direction is to realize that imagining a different economy does not need to be left to the economists, most of whom have trouble thinking differently about growth, productivity, or prosperity. The change process can begin with each of us just imagining what a new normal might entail. Environmental and economic justice activist Cylvia Hayes suggests that we begin with a few personal questions to spark that imagination:

- What kind of work would we like to do?
- How much would we like to work?
- Do we really need to drive to work every day?
- What kind of businesses would we like to see in our community?
- How and how much would we like to travel?
- Are we really OK with so much wealth in the hands of so few?
- Are we really OK with the ecological destruction that has been normalized?
- What actually makes us happy?[7]

The moral of the story is not that oil, chemical, airline, or car companies, or the many users of their products, are promoting business as usual with the intent to kill life-support systems on the planet. The evil is more banal than that; it involves giving priority to feeding economies that are widely believed to require growth and high corporate profits in order to function. That dubious economic story has made a few people rich and powerful enough to bend the fate of the entire planet to their misguided interests. It is time to at least imagine better economic and political ideas developed by a different cast of characters. A good place to start is with a critical look at the kind of thinking and communication that have limited our capacity to be both realistic and effective.

Language vs. Reality: Avoiding Solutions that Perpetuate Problems

Growing majorities in many nations want better solutions for environmental problems. However, there is danger that governments dominated by business concerns will not deliver much beyond feel-good plans. There have been some political successes on big problems in the past, such as shrinking the ozone hole and reducing auto emissions. However, most of the success stories involved relatively specific problems with clearer solutions. The complexity of the current crisis requires reimagining how developed societies can change basic aspects of industrial and agricultural production, transportation, investment, market regulation, consumption, and waste management. Solutions also involve thinking differently about economic development in poorer nations, starting with careful disconnection from global economies based on resource extraction and cheap labor and finding paths to more local production, saner resource management, and healthier communities.

A place to begin this journey is to learn from past episodes in which nice-sounding ideas fell short due to resistance to changing core economic beliefs and practices. A condensed history of the communication and politics of the global climate struggle since the 1950s is developed more in Chapters 2 and 3. For now, a brief sketch involves understanding how two important sets of ideas have meshed badly and delayed decisive economic and environmental action.

One set of ideas was spread by a movement of powerful business and political elites and neoliberal economists promoting free trade, privatization of public services, business deregulation, reducing labor and public welfare protections, and generally limiting the role of government in society. Following a massive global economic downturn during the

1970s, the world economy moved in a radically different direction with the rise of politicians like Ronald Reagan and Margaret Thatcher, who spread that new economic model of market deregulation and limited government discussed in Chapter 3.

During roughly the time period, as described in Chapter 2, a much larger but less powerful global citizens' environmental movement spread ideas about how the indiscriminate industrialization of the planet was endangering life. An iconic moment came in the United States in 1988 when James Hanson, a top climate scientist at the National Aeronautics and Space Administration, presented evidence in congressional testimony showing that human activity caused climate change. He told the Senate that "It is time to stop waffling so much and say that the evidence is pretty strong that the greenhouse effect is here."[8] He warned that the effects would reshape the earth for centuries to come.

Three decades later, Hanson concluded that despite growing awareness of the problems, no game-changing action had yet been taken.[9] Of course, there have been various improvements at the margins in terms of air or water quality, but the overall ecological condition is not good. Despite numerous big-picture policy initiatives and agreements, the results have produced more in the way of Green language than real substance.

Perhaps the most fateful compromise between the two grand sets of ideas pitting economic growth against sustainability was the fateful compromise of *sustainable development*. That lovely sounding phrase combines assumptions about economic growth, cheap resources, and expanding consumerism with promises to improve environmental conditions. The United Nations began to put the environment on its agenda at a conference in Stockholm in 1972, and later linked those discussions to the concerns of less developed nations that feared losing out in the new world economic order. A famous UN report published in 1987 (and discussed in Chapter 3) made *sustainable development* the triumphant, progressive-sounding political idea of its time. Many nations, both north and south, soon appointed sustainable development commissions that set about figuring out how to merge environmental protection with existing economic models – all at a time when the economy was globalizing, and many nations were joining the trends of shrinking government in favor of more market solutions for policy problems. The convergence of these factors has not gone well for the environment.

However, as political symbolism, sustainable development has been hard to beat. It is a perfect example of what Murray Edelman termed "words that succeed and policies that fail."[10] Few things are as appealing as communication that promises great things without requiring fundamental change or sacrifice. Despite, or more likely, because the idea was too good to be true, it quickly received broad political uptake. Most recently, a fanciful set of Sustainable Development Goals was adopted by the United Nations in 2015 and targeted for realization by 2030. The goals sound absolutely wonderful: ending poverty everywhere; ending hunger; ensuring healthy lives; access to education; gender equality; clean water and sanitation; access to energy that is affordable and sustainable; inclusive and sustainable economic growth (of at least 7 percent per annum in developing countries, and 3 percent globally); work for all; resilient infrastructure and sustainable industrialization; reducing inequality within and between countries; inclusive, safe, resilient, and sustainable cities; sustainable consumption patterns; urgent action against climate change; conserving oceans and marine resources; restoring and protecting terrestrial ecosystems; peaceful and inclusive societies; and strengthening global partnerships to promote these goals.[11]

The only way in which the contradictions of sustainable development could be resolved is through radically "decoupling" the material footprint of economic activity from economic growth. That means more technological innovations that requires less energy and resources to produce increasing outputs. The problem is that this has not happened. Although the material footprint of the global economy grew at a slower rate than world GDP toward the end of the last century, it still grew at an unsustainable rate. In this century, the resource burn has actually picked up, and in some models grown faster than GDP. Jason Hickel concludes that by any model, "global growth of 3% per year renders it empirically infeasible to achieve: (a) any reductions in aggregate global resource use, and (b) reductions in CO_2 emissions rapid enough to stay within the carbon budget for 2°C."[12] Most climate scientists, and the United Nations Paris agreement of 2015, regard a two-degree Celsius increase as the "no return" threshold, with 1.5 being a far less catastrophic goal, as noted earlier. As a result of the fatal pairing of sustainability and growth, today's levels of CO_2 have reached more than 400 parts per million, with 350 ppm generally regarded as the safe upper limit. That is more than a 40 percent rise in concentration since the beginning of the industrial revolution.[13] And half of that increase has come since 1988, when the story of sustainable development began.[14]

Life in an Age of Magical Thinking

The world of politics is full of magical thinking that invites us to hope that what we want to believe will somehow come true. Magical thinking generally ends up being too good to be true, as with that magical phrase sustainable development. Other forms of magical thinking include the long list of techno-fixes for environmental problems created by economies that work too well for the wealthy and powerful to really want them to change. One popular magical scheme is the idea of "scrubbing" the excess carbon dioxide out of the environment, as if the planet has developed issues with its heating and ventilation systems that some magical air filter can repair. A scheme that has attracted investments from Bill Gates and big oil companies involves building giant arrays of carbon dioxide scrubbers to remove CO2, and either pump it underground or somehow turn it into fuel. Many scientists have expressed skepticism about that plan, and government officials wonder who would pay the enormous costs.

In another magical moment, Gates was reported to be funding a Harvard science team to develop a technology for spreading millions of tons of chalk dust or other particles in the stratosphere to reflect and dim the sun. The idea stemmed from learning that the ash cloud from a massive volcanic eruption in the 1990s cooled the earth a bit for more than a year. Beyond the question of how this project would receive international approval, even the scientists involved admitted that it could have unknown effects on the atmosphere and weather, not to mention changing the sky under which we live. One of the team remarked "Our idea is terrifying ... But so is climate change."[15]

Another example of how business minds are magically grappling with mind-bending problems of saving both the planet and their business models, involves Amazon founder Jeff Bezos. The founder of the mega corporation has vowed to populate space with factories and workers to spare Earth more pollution, presumably from the runaway byproducts of consumerism driven by companies like his. However, after Amazon employees organized to raise awareness and do something about the company's large environmental footprint on earth, Bezos pledged $10 billion to fight climate change. One suspects that his climate fund will not go toward changing the company's business model of accelerated consumerism.

What seems clear, if we can look beyond the fog of denial, deception, and magical thinking is that we have evolved an economic system based on unsustainable growth and resource consumption, lethal toxic waste problems, and time horizons shortened by corporate profit calendars and increasing pressures to consume. The indiscriminate pursuit of growth is baked into core economic measures such as the Gross Domestic Product that counts the economic transactions involved with car accidents and toxic cleanups alongside building schools and taking care of the elderly as indicators of how well an economy is doing. This gospel of growth is spread by political and business elites and sanctified by economists, who act as the oracles of a secular religion. The mantras of growth echo across the news channels that provide the daily backdrop against which workers and consumers live their lives and calibrate their confidence in the future. With the advent of *surveillance capitalism* from tech firms such as Facebook and Google, consumerism is being pushed to new heights.[16]

The planetary economic binge has also led to great inequalities in wealth and power that increase the risk and stress of ordinary citizens and reduce their democratic voice, particularly in economic policy areas. Yet many in the growing "precariat" are also frightened by the warnings from business and political elites that environmental action will disrupt growth and cost jobs. While it is neither possible nor desirable just to replace economies that took many decades to evolve, it is possible to develop ideas about making orderly transitions and communicating them in less threatening ways.

What is currently missing are political communication processes that engage businesses, civic organizations, politicians, and voters in thinking about how to make transitions toward less damaging economic practices. The good news is that many people are able to see the seriousness of the situation we are in. Indeed, large populations are directly experiencing the realities of environmental damage through extreme weather events, coastal flooding, population migrations, toxic air, soil, food and water, related health problems, and images of ocean species choking on plastic. How can we move beyond denial or magical thinking and learn to think, communicate and act more realistically about these problems?

How Everyday Communication Logic Affects Thinking About Change

Communication is the human invention that lies at the center of our impact on the planet. People, from individuals to clashing civilizations, are fully engaged in sharing, enacting, or defeating ideas about who we are, how to live, and how to solve problems. We have even named this period of the earth's history – *the anthropocene* – for the impact that humans are having on the planet itself. Beyond naming things, there are many elemental aspects of communication that shape how we see and act in the world around us. In order to think differently about the uses of communication in making change, it helps to start with a few simple perspectives on more functional communication and politics.

Recognize That the Future Starts Now

You may have heard people say that the problem with managing future threats is that the present is compelling, and the future is abstract. Some even believe that humans are hard wired to live in the moment. There may be evidence for that, but there is also ample evidence showing that we are capable of planning, sacrificing, sharing, and caring. Since we have many choices in how to communicate about the current causes of our growing problems, a good place to start is by dissolving the artificial categorical distinction between present and future.

The causes of most environmental problems are happening now. Those problems mainly involve the basic workings and growing dysfunctions of current economics and politics. It is time to stop worrying about future unknowns such as imponderable "tipping points." It is time to stop pushing action into the future. Above all, it is time to realize that the current system is untenable. As Bill McKibben said way back in 2013, the future looks like 2012: heat, drought, floods, and historic storms. His conclusion: "We know how climate change ends; we now need to try and rewrite this future."[17]

Be Careful with Categories

The categories in which we place problems can make them easier or more difficult to solve. Our cognitive capacity to categorize and organize aspects of life into separate spheres often leads to what political scientist Murray Edelman described as "category mistakes."[18] A simple example of a category mistake is the assumption that if we want to solve environmental problems, we must stick to environmental solutions such as carbon taxes, phasing out coal, expanding renewable energy systems, or reducing the toxics in industrial processes. While these may seem like sensible ideas, they turn out to have magical properties because they all imply that we can just remove essential ingredients of entrenched, large-scale, global, economic activities and go on with our lives. Moreover, they limit our thinking to categories of solutions that continue to be promoted despite their records of failure to make enough difference.

Categorizing problems in environmental rather than economic terms leads to thinking about environmental solutions such as cleaning up various sorts of pollution, rather than addressing the sources of the problem. Without addressing the underlying economic sources of growing energy demands and emissions, efforts to control the output end of the problem will likely fall short. In addition, as discussed above, when categorized as primarily environmental concerns, political efforts typically run into the more powerful category of economic arguments that limit the possibilities for more fundamental transformation. Working within such imagined category limits results in winning a few battles for carbon taxes, coal phase-outs, or Green energy schemes, while continuing to lose the larger war for more sustainable societies.

There is a large academic field dedicated to environmental communication, but most of it addresses ways to frame and target messages to particular audiences about specific environmental problems. In his excellent review and synthesis of this vast literature, Maxwell Boykoff notes the advantages of venturing beyond narrow environmental themes to engage with often decisive questions of economics. He notes, for example, that in 1930 John Maynard Keynes wrote a book with the evocative title *Economic Possibilities for our Grandchildren* and suggested that we begin thinking about the mix of "equity, power, access, and values" required for long-term sustainability "at the human-environment interface." [19] The point being that complex problems require intersectional thinking.

Learn to Think at the Intersection of Categories

We can think and act differently by categorizing environmental problems in economic and political terms. This may lead to understanding the causes and solutions differently. Learning to communicate at the intersection of different categories (e.g. environment, economics, and politics) provides better understanding of complex issues. For example, if we think about what makes a great athlete, we naturally include aspects from different categories such as age, strength, agility, height, weight, motivation, skills, and conditioning, among others. It would be difficult to describe and compare athletic ability without using multiple categories, each containing different relevant properties.

Despite the capacity to think at the intersections of categories about many everyday life spheres such as sports, most discussions of environmental problems are often limited by narrow categorical thinking, such as alarming reports of increased carbon dioxide levels, or schemes for reducing the problem at the output end by taxing or capturing carbon. *Intersectional communication* combines economic, political, and environmental elements to better grasp the underlying problems and more effective solutions. We will see that this simple shift in perspective enables us to discover that most environmental problems are really economic and political in nature.

Avoid Backwards Thinking that Gets Us Working the Wrong Ends of Problems

Magical thinking keeps people hoping that things can go on as before with more attention to cleaning up the toxic economic byproducts such as removing plastic from oceans, while we produce ever more plastic, or shifting to renewable energy even as overall energy demand continues to increase reliance on fossil fuels. One lesson we can learn from the logic of treating symptoms, rather than the underlying economic dysfunction producing them, is that gains in treating symptoms often lead to growth of the underlying problems. This is called a "rebound effect," meaning that gains in technology or efficiency may be eaten up by increased demand. A simple example is the logic of solving traffic congestion by building more freeways. The result is generally to put more traffic on the roads, and to create more congestion that spreads farther out. Maybe creating better public transit options and working more from home would be less backwards. In many areas, from mobility to energy, the goal of decoupling material footprints from economic productivity discussed above has not produced the promised results.

Consider how we typically talk about plastics: wild schemes to clean up ocean plastics or figuring out how to make recycling actually work. Meanwhile, plastic wastes continue to grow. We might think, instead, about political and economic arrangements that change how we produce, package, transport, and consume products. If we indulge the imagination still further, we may permit ourselves to think about more distributed and localized production that moves away from giant industrial corporations that profit from wasteful practices because they need to produce huge volumes of products, ship them great distances, and then encourage consumers to discard them and buy more. Perhaps we can find ways to reward local production based on less waste and transportation energy.

Here's a wicked thought: what if plastic objects floating in the oceans are not the only or even the most serious part of the plastic problem? Dozens of toxic chemicals are released into the environment in the manufacturing process and baked into products only to leach out during use and decomposition. There are rising levels of microplastic particles in our air, water, and food chains from the degradation of objects and the washing of fibers from clothes, cleansing products, and other sources. The ingestion of microplastic may do more harm to life forms than the large objects we now worry about cleaning up. Moral of the story: the logic of cleaning up plastics is backwards. More energy could be spent on how we package, contain, ship, and promote products.

Finally, consider the backwards thinking fallacies in how people typically talk about renewable energy. For starters, such talk seldom addresses the rebound effects of growing energy consumption that outpaces the benefits of renewables. In the decade from 2008 to 2018, renewable energy sources grew at faster rates than fossil-based sources. That is generally considered a good thing. Unfortunately, the growth in total global energy demand outpaced renewables, so there was no net gain on the carbon emissions.[20] To the contrary, the burning of coal, the worst fossil fuel, increased by roughly 75 percent in the first decade of this century, and reached a plateau at about 40 percent of global energy in the period from 2010 to 2020. This slowing reflects many coal plants being taken offline in the US and western Europe.[21] However, the use of coal in Asia remains strong, and hundreds of new plants are being built in China and India. Australia and China have branded cleaner coal as Green policies.

Even where the use of coal has ended, the transition generally moves to natural gas, which is only less terrible. What comes after natural gas? That depends on how we imagine our underlying economic practices. Since discussions of renewables are seldom linked to underlying economic logics, continued growth of demand for fossil fuels amid all the talk of renewables has pushed CO_2 levels over the recognized safe levels of 350 parts per million, to over 400, and rising, as noted above. The last time such levels existed was several millions of years ago, and sea levels were dramatically higher. Even conservative projections of sea level rise involve large percentages of the earth's coastal population being displaced, most with no place to go. The tropics will become uninhabitable due to a combination of heat, disease, and food and water shortages. Those who do not perish will join population migrations that will make those of today seem small, as the World Bank estimates over 140 million climate migrants will be seeking refuge in the next thirty years.[22]

What is important to remember is that the extent of these disruptions can still be managed. But we need to stop communicating with logics that address the wrong end of the problem. Even most of the articles from which the above data were drawn continue calling for output reductions.[23] Perhaps it is time to start changing our political communication logics so that we can talk more about economic inputs and core values?

Notice How Facts and Values Are Used Selectively to Support Each Other

Values reveal what people think of as more and less important in their lives. The categorization of problems may also signal something about values underlying an argument or claim. Most of us value our jobs and want an economy that works well. As a result, just raising the fear that environmental action will cost jobs or hurt the economy may dampen popular support for environmental solutions. In these ways, communication evokes value conflicts that render citizens unsure about what to do, and become "quiescent," or accepting frustrating situations, to use another idea from Murray Edelman. [24] In this way, the values embedded in category choices may be used to justify political inaction on the environment and reinforce the unhelpful value of economy first.

Evidence is often brought into or left out of arguments to shore up the separation between artificially constructed value categories. For example, claims that environmental action will damage the economy are often made as if they are self-evidently true. Often, little or no evidence is offered to support such claims, or to see if different qualities of work are available in Greener industries. In some cases, people do present evidence, but there is precious little testing or critical examination to see how well different facts hold up. Spotting the selective uses of evidence to support values can then help spot logical weaknesses in arguments.

This does not mean we should mistrust evidence. Far from it. What it does mean is that we should be careful to strengthen what we value with smarter category choices, and then compare the evidence for different sides of the argument. Environmentalists are clearly winning the evidence game but losing the political game for lack of ability to communicate in ways that level the playing field with categories, values and facts that support different economic activities. One place to begin is to understand that current economic practices are not the only possible ones, or even the best ones. Perhaps different economic schemes better adapted to regional conditions would be more consistent with things that people value: secure work, more free time, less stress, more community-based businesses, products built to last, and an emphasis on social and environmental value over maximizing profits. There is remarkably thin support among ordinary people for many core features of the current economic system. Not surprisingly, those who value and promote it and select the facts to make their cases are largely the ones who profit most. Since those arguments invite us to accept the underlying systems as natural or at least inevitable, many people, including many activists, are inclined to settle for "being realistic" and tinkering around the edges in all the ways that have turned out not to be enough.

Think Critically about "Being Realistic"

Many hopes for change are dashed on the rocks of "being realistic." What is realistic turns out to be what influential people promote, what is most likely to be taken up politically, and what can be grafted onto existing institutionalized aspects of our everyday lives. When civil-society organizations try to be "realistic" in order to get funding, or to be granted seats at the bargaining table, they may end up perpetuating the very systems they are trying to change. Above all, "being realistic" means that a good deal of our political communication reflects the institutions that structure it, and the resulting communication ends up reproducing those institutional structures.

The result is that much of the environmental communication we hear focuses on fixing isolated output problems such as trying to save endangered species or reducing carbon dioxide levels. That is partly because of the political processes that have developed to handle routine policy problems reduce environmental issues to fragmentary parts of the whole. This fracturing of environmental action becomes even more limiting when political advocates continue to categorize their issues in environmental terms rather than talking about their economic and political roots.

These dilemmas were well described by John Lanchester in his review of two books: *The Uninhabitable Earth* by David Wallace-Wells and *Losing Earth* by Nathaniel Rich. The first of those books points out the failures of many environmental actions such as efforts to reduce carbon dioxide. The second book marvels that we are having essentially the same political discussions now as thirty years ago, when the alarming rise of CO_2 gained scientific and popular attention (recall the earlier story about the great compromise of sustainable development). In response to this puzzling situation, Lanchester framed the political challenge succinctly:

> Our politics, our societies, are arranged around individual and group interests. These interests have to do with class, or ethnicity, or gender, or economics – make your own list. By asserting these interests, we call out to each other so that

> as a collective we see and hear one another ... The problem with climate change as an existential threat to humanity, is that the interest-based model of politics and society doesn't work. Most of the people in whose interest we are demanding action aren't there. They haven't been born yet. And because the areas first and most affected by climate change are the poorest regions of earth, we are talking about the least seen, least represented group on our planet.[25]

Given that being realistic is keeping us on the path to ever greater life disruptions, is the alternative to be unrealistic? Of course not. We can simply imagine different realities. That is how most serious change generally starts. Most ideas that ended up producing fundamental change were dismissed initially as unrealistic.

Using Communication Logics to Decode Everyday Communication

Even smart, thoughtful people may select particular categories and facts to implicitly promote particular values and focus the logic of their arguments. If arguments are constructed cleverly, we may not even notice the values or the faulty logics because we are impressed by the marshalling of facts, or because we hope that the underlying organization of our worlds does not need to change. For example, Bill Gates has proclaimed Steven Pinker's book *Enlightenment Now* as "my favorite book of all time."[26] Pinker, a Harvard psychology professor and author of popular books on the human condition, offers impressive data showing that humans today are better off than at any time in history. Among some of Gates' favorite factoids from *Enlightenment Now* are these: you're 37 times less likely to be killed by lightning than a century ago thanks to better weather forecasting; we spend ten fewer hours a week doing laundry than in 1920; we are less likely to die on the job; we are living longer, earning more, and we are even getting smarter!

So why are "we" not all celebrating? In an interview with Gates, Pinker blames depressing news coverage for clouding the far happier realities of our modern lives. It is easy to agree that the news is depressing. And there is much to be said for being optimistic. But one can easily find sharp critiques of the Gates–Pinker data, and other equally impressive empirical arguments that lead to far less rosy conclusions than those produced by Pinker and Gates, among others.[27]

There are still many arguments like the Gates–Pinker discussion that seem to be objectively based on facts. But it turns out that values and their related emotions (likes, wants, loves, hates, fears) are what generally motivate us to seek and share information in the first place.[28] Emotions both stem from and help define the values that make us who we are, and guide us in finding others we want to associate with or avoid. Without these emotional centering principles, we would be lost and confused, and unable to decide what information is worth seeking and sharing.

Let's return to the claims by Bill Gates and Steven Pinker that "we never had it so good." This sounds like an evidence-driven argument, and on the surface, it is. This is where the underlying logic of the argument must be decoded a bit more. It is not immediately clear what particular values are being promoted beyond simply "enlightening" ourselves about our true condition. By many of the measures cited by Pinker, Gates, and other techno-optimists, private life seems to be looking better for more people. But measurable improvements on a list of individual indicators do not mean that people are necessarily better off collectively. For example, what if more jobs and better wages come along with the growth of megacities, severe air pollution, declining water quality, lack of housing, and poor sanitation? Or, what if the continued global spread of consumerism that has created more jobs and better wages also escalates the depletion of resources and the introduction of more wastes and toxins into the environment? These considerations were not featured in the Gates–Pinker conversation, which focused on particular ways of categorizing progress, supported by evidence neatly matched to the categories. And, without saying so, those categorizations of progress and selections of evidence implicitly invite the audience to see the value of the current economic system that has produced those definitions and measures of prosperity.

The prominence and media access of people like Gates and Pinker overshadow the publicity given to possibly more attractive ideas about what it means to prosper, based less on wealth and technology, and more on leisure time, community, happiness, health, and better distribution of resources. Such issues aside, Gates often sounds progressive in his efforts to grapple with various social, health, and environmental problems. As noted earlier, he is putting some of his fortune behind businesses developing technologies to strip CO_2 from the atmosphere.[29] Although there is little evidence that such solutions would work, even if they could be financed at massive scale, this emotionally satisfying techno-vision enables the environmental solution to be categorized in a way that preserves Gates' argument that the current economy is working great for us. This all adds up to a conclusion that there is no need to change the system that has made Gates one of the richest individuals in human history – beyond tinkering with a few marginal issues such as inequality, health, education, and that pesky CO_2.

Beyond neatly separating the economic system from the environment, thinking like this also puts a great deal of emphasis on a single set of environmental problems: global warming and the problem of fossil fuels and carbon. What if this overarching focus on greenhouse gases may actually reduce our attention from the large list of other environmental problems that stem from the same underlying economic practices? By thinking in separate environmental problem categories, and putting the emphasis on warming, most of those other challenges (e.g. other forms of chemical pollution) will persist, even if the pace of warming is slowed down. What remains largely unchanged is the economic system. For example, a study funded by the US National Aeronautics and Space Administration modeled multiple factors affecting the quality of future life, including a host of other environmental toxins, population pressures, climate warming, resource consumption, waste processing, socioeconomic inequality, consumer lifestyles, water quality, and energy. The studies predicted a catastrophic civilization collapse if future scenarios proceed on anything like their current paths.[30]

Decoding discussions such as the exchange between Gates and Pinker requires understanding that while reason and evidence are surely better than lies and deception, they are often deployed in the service of particular values. Gates is a leading booster of the current form of capitalism, and why wouldn't he be, since it has made him one of the richest people in history? So, it is hardly surprising that he and many others are trying to prop up that system by mobilizing facts that make a case that it is working well for everyone, perhaps with a few adjustments here or there. At the same time, it is difficult to ignore the relative gap between four dollars a day for the average Indian, and the astounding fortune that the same system has generated for Gates.

The above concerns aside, Gates is admirable for giving away a large part of his fortune to improve health and education and encouraging other multi-billionaires to do the same. But Gates is also the quintessential Davos Man: a member of the global elite that gathers in the exclusive Swiss ski resort of Davos most every winter to share ideas about keeping global free-market capitalism working with a human touch. Thus, it is not surprising that Gates and most of his peers continue to discuss economics and environment as though they can both continue along much the same paths with some tinkering here and there.

Why So Much Everyday Communication Is Unhelpful

The point of the above discussion is that more productive ways of approaching the environmental crisis are sidetracked by how we typically communicate about it. Like Bill Gates, many people in positions of power and authority tend to separate environmental and economic spheres, resulting in focusing attention on marginal solutions such as carbon taxes or massive deployment of carbon dioxide scrubbers. Yet, when talk about changing the basic functioning of the economy is removed from the conversation, there is little chance that the remaining room for action will make much difference. For many people, imagining how to change the economy seems both overwhelming and frightening. These fears of change add to the reception of emotionally reassuring arguments for improvement at the margins, or for doubling down on unworkable ideas such as sustainable development.

The introduction of better ideas into the popular imagination is further challenged by a fragmenting media system that enables – and algorithmically prompts – people to seek information that confirms their own feelings about things. As a result, much of what people find is unhelpful for thinking clearly about how to live better within the life-support capacities of the planet. The next section illustrates some common features of our everyday communication environments, which we can learn to navigate more effectively. The growing dissonance of much contemporary political communication should further motivate those seeking change to better coordinate efforts to develop ideas that can be amplified enough to cut through the noise.

Few people dig deeply into conversations such as the one between Steven Pinker and Bill Gates, but most people do spend a lot of time with various media that carry information and images of life on the planet. If we think about what is popular, shared, liked, and influential, relatively few people are exposed to attractive alternatives to their present realities. Most communication environments marginalize creative visions about how to live differently – unless that is already your thing, and you find social-media networks for that. With few exceptions, most everyday communication is designed to keep us in the moment, focused on what is happening now. Most of us are enmeshed in communication environments involving media platforms such as Facebook, Instagram, WhatsApp, Twitter, Google, or YouTube. Those communication services are "free" only because they host underlying algorithms that prompt us to buy, consume, feed our sensory impulses, and share constant updates on our social networks. In short, life in the tech age moves fast and stays in the now. Even discussions of the future are near term: the next election, the next economic report, or ad placements nudging our interest in the next vacation destination.

Thanks to social and digital media, much of what we do and communicate is recorded, stored, cross referenced, and used to channel our attention and behavior. This surveillance system is fed by our phones, computers, and "smart" devices at home, that help behavior modification algorithms learn who our friends are, what we buy, where we go, what websites we visit, how much time we spend on them, what we click, like, share, and even the topics of conversations we have in our homes. The communication algorithms that feed in and out of central aspects of our lives are, for the most part, designed to keep us buying more stuff, and, during elections, voting for particular parties or candidates.

There is not much business value in content that is not constantly activating our short-term attention and behavior. As I write these words, the most shared image, ever, on Instagram is a simple picture of a chicken egg, which has attracted more than fifty million likes at the time of this writing. The egg, named Eugene, eclipsed Kylie Jenner's previous record, following the birth announcement of her child. Eugene quickly gained more than ten million followers, and even starred in a video on Hulu. It is unlikely that such large numbers will buzz about the alignment of environment, economy, and democracy on Instagram – unless those already concerned about the planetary future get together and develop more sharable ideas, images, and memes that travel.

Let's reconsider consumerism in this context. If you ask whether it makes sense for billions of consumers to constantly upgrade and refresh their novelties, just to obey fashion propaganda, or feed their own Facebook behavior modification algorithms, most people would likely say no. Yet, consumer industries dedicated to fashion, entertainment, travel, and other pursuits have found ever more effective ways to communicate trendy images to the cool kids. Communication in the form of advertising propaganda even helps us imagine not being happy without the churn of consumer novelties. Advertising fantasies encourage us to stay in the now, in a timeless world of newer, bigger, better, faster stuff that is cool enough "to die for." Needless to say, those communication realities make the environmental, economic, and human costs of consumerism disappear. Life represented in the branded world is free of environmental collapse, unhappy sweatshops, and (save for anti-perspirant and anti-depressant ads) lonely people.

Justin Lewis has discussed these timeless and disconnected commercial media logics in a compelling book *Beyond Consumer Capitalism: Media and the Limits to Imagination*.[31] The Media Education Foundation produced a film based on the book, in which Lewis opened with this overview: I'm going to talk about our dominant economic, social, cultural, political system: consumer capitalism. At the heart of the success of this model lie two linked ideas. The first is an image of "the good life" based on the accumulation of consumer goods, and the second is the idea of perpetual and infinite economic growth. What I want to argue today is that both those ideas are beginning to unravel, and that there are a new set of conditions in the twenty-first century, which means that consumer capitalism may be past its sell-by date.[32] While this may be true, it would not be apparent in the daily flows of commercial images pushed by the algorithms of Google, Facebook, Instagram, YouTube, and other media platforms.

Despite signing away the rights to our personal data so those companies can better influence how we behave and how we attach feelings to outside realities, we do have a kind of perverse individual choice over what versions of reality we prefer. If we want to hear that climate change is a hoax, such communication is easily available. Or, if we want to understand more scientific explanations for why the ice is melting and life is threatened, we can dial that in as well. And the more we visit sites that appeal to us, the more we will be invited to attend to more of the same. But these kinds of communication do not help transcend polarization or better address our existential problems. Welcome to life in the filter bubble.

Beyond finding better ideas as individuals, it is important to learn how more positive visions can be developed and shared by organizations, amplified across dense social-media networks, and better positioned for political uptake when opportunities arise. Most change in democracies depends on mobilizing voting publics to pressure political parties to introduce better ideas into elections and policy processes. The first step is to use the communication logics presented in this chapter to begin imagining the kind of change we want.

Imagining a Different World

It is difficult to navigate the high volumes of noise about the current crisis and figure out what positions make sense. A good place to start is by figuring out how each of us experiences life at the intersections of environment, economy, society, and politics. Putting ourselves in the picture does not have to be complicated. In fact, it may be as simple as literally drawing pictures of the world we feel we live in, contrasted with the one we would like to inhabit.

Consider the appealing vision of Kate Raworth, an ecological economist in the UK, who has adapted a long history of thinking about circular or steady state economics into an easy to understand image of "doughnut economics." In her view, the basic wellbeing of people comes first. These developmental basics are drawn on the inner rings of the doughnut, and include such things as food, water, energy, health care, housing, decent work with livable incomes, access to communication and quality information, all operating in political cultures that favor gender equality, social justice, and political voice.[33] These inner social and economic rings of the doughnut must operate within the outer rings of environmental resources and limits. In developing her visual image, Raworth avoids jargon and polarizing categorizations. She invites everyone to develop their own visualizations to help imagine how our worlds look and feel. I have taken up this invitation to visualize the intersection of economy, society, politics, and environment.

First, let's begin with how public officials and conventional media typically invite people to imagine our currently constructed economic, social, political, and environmental realities. It is difficult to amass precise data on how the complex realities around us are represented in the news, popular books, movies, and other communication, but it is possible to offer impressions as a communication scholar who has long studied these things. Figure 1.1 shows a visualization of what I take to be the most common media representations of these intersecting life spheres. Think of it as a visual hypothesis that can be measured for different publics engaged with different media systems.

Beyond the passing episodes of human crisis such as wars and natural disasters, the daily news is regularly filled with messages about the economy: how the stock markets are doing, employment rates, consumer confidence, and all-important growth reports and projections. These themes also run through political campaigns, business reports, and everyday conversations. In so much of our communication, the economy seems to be our biggest and most important life sphere. Even during the Covid-19 pandemic, understandable attention was focused on the economic future, but less of that concern was devoted to how to bring engines of prosperity more in line with the environment than how to return to the old normal.

Next comes the world of politics through news about parties, politicians, policies, conflicts, scandals, elections, debates, and protest movements. But when it comes to the economy, politics is typically represented as the sphere of human activity entrusted in managing the current system. Politicians are held accountable to how well they do that, and their performance is typically measured in terms of growth, jobs, inflation, and other indicators. In this sense, our political imagination is also limited by the existing economic sphere. This is why politics is represented in Figure 1.1 as operating largely within established economic boundaries, rather than the other way around.

Next come portrayals of social life, from travel and lifestyle features to seemingly chronic problems of hunger, migration, homelessness, health, education, and other aspects of wellbeing. The degree to which social welfare is well maintained by economies and politics varies from one place to another. In many nations, social issues are unevenly addressed, and so the social sphere often spills outside of economic and political boundaries. Even so-called wealthy or prosperous societies such as the United States have created serious levels of homelessness, precarious jobs, uneven health care, and poor education. Social welfare is much better in some nations than others, but nearly everywhere, some numbers of people fall outside the basic protections of economy and politics.

And, last but not least, the dominant representations of the world that I have experienced in mainstream media, involve business and political elites paying little more than lip service to environmental values. Indeed, most reporting portrays a struggling environment, dominated by all the other spheres, with few signs that those other spheres are operating within environmental limits. The reader, of course, may have different imaginations of these spheres. A starting point for trying to get our visions on the same page is to imagine and compare them. I invite the reader to draw her own picture of our current realities.

The next question is: How might all of this look in a more perfect world? As a thought exercise, or an "imaginary," consider how we might live if the environment were the largest concern on which all else depends. And then imagine that we organize societies in terms of environmental capacities to support them. (This may require changing how we think about our responsibilities to each other as planetary citizens.) Next, imagine how it would be if politics

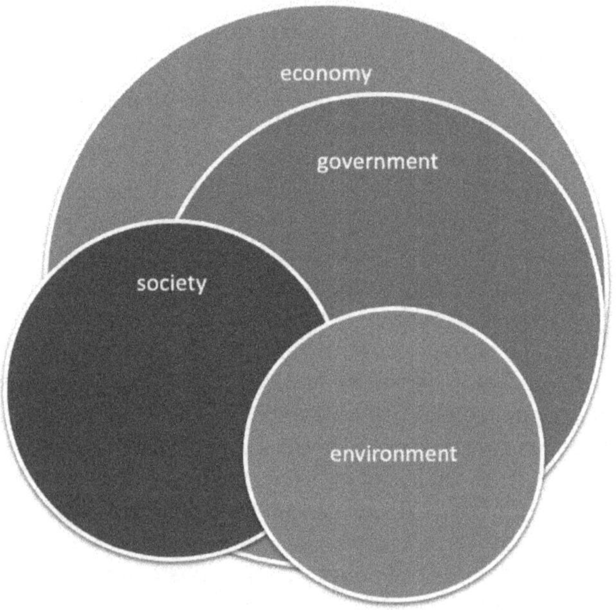

Figure 1.1 Visualizing Typical Media Representations of Current Human Life Spheres

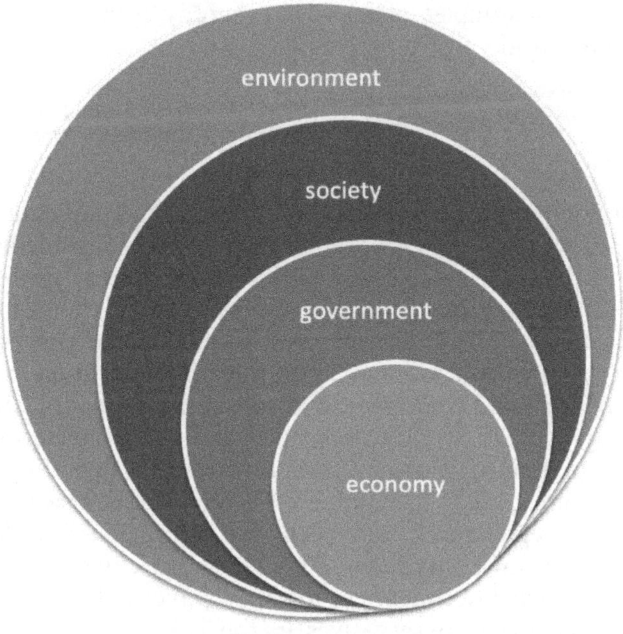

Figure 1.2 A Different Human Imaginary

(politicians, interests, movements, parties, elections) actually answered more broadly to societies that were more attuned to caring for the planet. Finally, imagine an economy that is organized by politics that are more accountable to society and environment. Figure 1.2 illustrates this vision that animates much of the thinking in the book.

Both Figures 1.1 and 1.2 show how using communication logics can help us better understand both current dilemmas and future possibilities. For example, we often hear politicians operating from their economically subordinate positions in Figure 1.1 saying that it would be nice to adopt tougher environmental policies but that the costs are too high in terms of economic disruption and, that often-fatal word, "jobs". If we look to Figure 1.2, however, we can imagine more politicians asking how we can create jobs and good lives within what we know to be the limits of the environment. That is a very different way of thinking and acting. Now, let's use these background perspectives to help decode some examples of familiar everyday communication about our world.

The Politics Problem

If lucid communication about the future is made difficult by the hyper-personalized algorithms of social media, something similar has happened to our politics. To varying degrees, parties and governments in many democratic nations have been captured by business interests preaching the gospel of economic growth and minimum government intervention in the economy. It should come as little surprise that communication was involved in these developments as well. A popular story sold to voters in most democracies toward the end of the last century promised that unchaining business from the shackles of government regulation would mean greater individual freedom in the form of lower taxes and more consumer choice.

As described briefly above, the first wave of free-market mania came from conservatives in the late 1970s eager to liberate business interests from the taxes and regulation of the Keynesian economic regime that emerged during the Great Depression and became consolidated after World War II. However, by the 1990s, even politicians on the center left (e.g. Bill Clinton, Tony Blair, Gerhard Schroeder) promoted economic globalization, reduced government regulation, and market solutions for public policy problems. The continuing popularity of dealing with environmental problems with carbon taxes or "cap and trade" market swaps for emissions are legacies of this thinking. The result is that many basic economic alternatives that organized earlier eras of politics have been taken out of circulation. The result is more limited voter choices in areas of employment security, living wage, and the quality of public services from energy and transportation, to health and education. Such issues that defined mid twentieth-century democratic politics were replaced by propaganda about the wonders of market solutions, and the moral code of individuals taking responsibility for their own social welfare.

With the erosion of meaningful economic choice, party differences began to shrink, and politics became increasingly like consumer communication, with parties resorting to advertising slogans and marketing to try to sell brand images to increasingly disillusioned voters.[34] This hollowing out of parties and governments is what Colin Crouch has termed *post-democracy*.[35] It is not surprising that the hollowing of democracy has resulted in growing disillusionment with politics and economics. As the economic benefits of the last forty years of growth have been distributed increasingly upward, and most jobs have become less secure and attractive, trust levels in government and parties have gone down steadily. European trust and confidence levels in parties and governments had fallen to around 35 percent on average before the Covid-19 pandemic.[36] As the promise of free-market prosperity turned into wage stagnation, austerity, and debt, the general disaffection with mainstream politics has turned to political anger. However, that anger has taken different forms on the far left and the far right.[37]

The radical left has disconnected notably from parties and elections over this period and turned more toward local, direct, participatory democracy, punctuated with occasional massive protests against generally deteriorating conditions. Growing skepticism about the legitimacy of Social Democratic and Labor parties has fueled the ongoing fragmentation of issues and causes, accentuating the lack of widely shared visions of change that were once developed and channeled through parties and ideologies. While the emerging left culture of diversity, inclusiveness, direct democracy, and localism has been vibrant and interesting, it is not helping chart a new course at higher levels of politics and policy.

Meanwhile, the radical right has grown into large movements that have successfully fed their anger into a variety of new and rebranded parties. The political communication networks feeding in and out of those movements and parties have spread denial and disinformation about climate change, immigration, and other topics that mobilize voters who feel traditional identities and ways of life slipping away. Many of the ideological divides of the past century have been displaced by identity politics and emotional clashes over race, immigration, religion, sexual rights, and struggles over who are the true national citizens. If change is possible in this environment, more effective models of political communication are required.

The many strands of environmental activism come together in mass demonstrations to sound alarms or call for stronger agreements at climate summits, but many citizens and movement factions often disagree on deeper economic agendas or common political strategies. The challenge is to figure out how to gain agreement on broader visions for change and organize more effective communication around them. Until more environmental organizations, economic justice groups and democratic reform advocates join forces around ideas at the intersections of their issue category differences, they will continue being friendly competitors rather than solidary allies advancing popular agendas of more fundamental change.

There is little to lose by seeing if we could do more for environmental problems by inserting somewhat larger ideas – such as steady state, circular, or "doughnut" economics – more centrally into the environmental conversation and move beyond routine politics. The challenge is to find ideas and strategies that bridge organizations in environment, economic and democratic reform movements, and engage publics and politicians. The overarching question guiding the rest of the book is: *What kinds of communication, combined with what forms of organized political power, will enable shared vision of political and economic transformation to develop?*

The answers to this broad question involve expanding the study and practice of communication beyond focusing on isolated concepts such as framing messages, setting public and media agendas, or modeling networks. These and other basic elements of communication must be combined to understand how information flows in society to unite or divide, to bridge diverse networks or stop at their boundaries, and to better connect publics and politicians in gaining political uptake, resulting in effective change.

The Idea-Flow Framework

Ideas can matter a great deal in our lives, but they matter less when sitting on lonely websites, or trapped in tiny organizations, or when they compete with hundreds of other ideas shouted by protesters in noisy demonstrations. Yet most of the realities we live with, or protest angrily against, began with ideas produced by academics, theologians, advertisers, politicians, and more than a few ordinary people. The question is whether there is anything special that distinguishes ideas that become dominant, from the many more, and possibly even better, ideas that go nowhere. How ideas develop and flow in society has interested many observers, from students of social movements, organizations, and networks, to communication practitioners, who market and advertise products from soaps to politicians. It is not surprising that there is no single model of how ideas flow because there are so many different contexts that differently define the topic. However, there are some helpful starting points.

Communication scholar Manuel Castells created a body of insightful work about the transformation of societies from group-based structures to more flexible networked organizations. Among other things, he talked about networked idea flows that join large protest networks in global action. His analyses showed that the mechanisms affecting the flows of ideas can alter the ways in which we experience time and space. Those alterations in time and space are partly due to properties of the web, with its distributed, end-to-end architecture, and the many connected platforms and devices that enable extremely fast transmission, asynchronous engagement, streaming live and on demand, and the portability of the many devices that connect us. Those time-and-space-changing technologies affect the flow of ideas and action, often with remarkable results, such as enabling the largest coordinated transnational public protests in human history that have occurred in this century. In many of these cases, the information flows that connect and disconnect people are organic and not always centrally managed. This makes it all the more remarkable that the complex networks in massive mobilizations may display learning, adaptation, and rapid mobilization of large numbers of people.[38]

My own work with Alexandra Segerberg shows how technology-enabled crowds can mirror some of the behavior routines that commonly define formal organizations, often with much less traditional leadership and fewer resources.[39] While these vast networks have done surprising things, from bringing down governments, to drawing attention to political problems, they are also limited. For one thing, technologically networked crowds form most easily under two conditions. The first pattern involves single issues that many people have experienced personally, such as the kinds of violations of basic individual rights and protections that prompted #MeToo or #BlackLivesMatter. The second pattern involves protest agendas that are open to many different causes associated with a general problem, as happened in the Occupy Wall Street protests of 2011–2012, when millions of people shared different stories under the protest frame: We Are The 99%. The massive environmental protests in recent years also fit this pattern. These networked protests reflect the ethos of diversity and inclusiveness that has characterized much of the left in the digital age, keeping most of those mass gatherings from consolidating into more coherent movements.

The unmanaged spread of ideas in loosely structured networks is not well suited for the kind of agenda building required to address environmental and economic issues. As crowd-enabled networks try to address complex intersectional problems, it becomes difficult to coordinate and manage flows of ideas that often change as they travel across different networks. Alexandra Segerberg, Yunkang Yang, and I have examined how ideas travel in complex network ecologies that lack much organizational coordination.[40] We found that even relatively like-minded crowds can dramatically filter and alter ideas as they cross over multiple networks from central sources to more peripheral publics. For example, the Occupy Wall Street protests in the US involved a lot of different ideas coming from many diverse individuals and organizations. We were able to identify the main ideas being promoted from the social-media accounts of core activists and see what happened as those ideas traveled across different supporter networks on their way to broad public distribution. We found that concerns at the core of the protests about changing the banking system and fixing democracy became gradually replaced by understandings on the periphery that the protests were mainly about economic inequality. Inequality was among many ideas circulating in protest networks, but it was more easily circulated among networks on the periphery that had already given considerable attention to that problem.

One lesson from studying idea flows in loosely organized networks is that organizations can be important in stabilizing and focusing them. Even if contemporary networked societies are less responsive to traditional forms of organizational leadership, Dave Karpf has shown that more flexible, hybrid organizations are important for monitoring idea flows and helping to focus messages and related actions.[41] Bruce Bimber, Andrew Flanagin, and Cynthia Stohl have shown that traditional membership organizations face challenges in networked societies due to changing preferences about how people choose to connect with issues and causes that matter to them. Some organizations have been better able than others to adjust their missions and uses of technologies to engage publics.[42]

Organizations that have become more flexible in terms of thinking about spreading their ideas are also better positioned to enable and join larger idea networks with other organizations. Alexandra Segerberg and I have termed this kind of structuring of large-scale idea and action networks *organizationally enabled connective action*.[43] This form of networked organization has proven particularly effective in targeted issue and protest campaigns such as the #PutPeopleFirst global protests following the global economic crisis of 2008, or the Robin Hood Tax campaign, which pressed for taxing financial speculation in a number of EU member states. Those, and many similar campaigns, involved different organizations stepping back from trying to brand or own the action and developing networking technologies to enable other organizations and individuals to become active participants in sharing ideas.

While organizationally enabled connectivity can be highly effective in time-and-goal-limited campaigns, it is less clear how to motivate the people and organizations involved to develop more enduring idea-action networks for long-term economic and environmental change. A related next question about idea flows is what motivates people and organizations to connect to diverse networks and at the same time to join in building, reinforcing, and sharing common-core ideas? An interesting area of research is the study of goal clarification and alignment in different kinds of networks ranging over formal organizations, group meetings, and city infrastructures for transportation, communication, or housing. Computer scientist Alex Pentland has examined how ideas and related behavior patterns flow (or don't) in these settings, based on how people respond to social pressures and incentives to explore new networks and engage with their ideas.[44] Pentland was interested in designing relatively focused social applications that help people have better meetings, manage organizations more effectively, or build cities that people can navigate more easily. Our variation on this perspective involves understanding what kinds of push-and-pull incentives can help bridge different networks of environmental, new economy, and political reform organizations to motivate development of more common goals and strategies? And how can more coherent movements help shape communication between citizens and politicians?

Taking these different perspectives on idea flows into account, the question becomes how diverse networks concerned about environment, economy, and democracy can better coordinate the production, and manage the spread of ideas about a different political economy? Beyond better coordinating the production of ideas, it is also important to understand how they can be packaged to travel over different kinds of stakeholder networks: academics, the press, organizations in different movement sectors, concerned citizens with worries about work and lifestyle; businesses concerned about risk and uncertainty; and politicians who must find ways to address diverse stakeholders. Then we should think about how those networks can connect in ways that amplify shared understandings in order to position those ideas for political uptake in elections and policy processes.

The model developed and applied throughout the book involves learning how to better crystallize and promote political goals through processes that focus on idea *production*, *packaging*, *networked sharing*, and *political uptake*. Each of these elements is crucial, and they all operate together to determine which ideas gain what kind of standing, in which social and institutional circles, and with what impact on life conditions. This framework can be used both to understand how ideas travel in various social and political networks, and as a practical guide for designing communication for change.

Idea Production

There are many different kinds of idea producers. Sometimes ordinary individuals produce powerful ideas. Consider the case of Greta Thunberg. As a sixteen-year-old student in Sweden, she decided to make a one-person strike for climate change by leaving school and protesting outside the Swedish Parliament building in August of 2018. She held a hand-painted sign that said: "school strike for climate." Her idea was amplified by media attention, and other students soon joined her vigil. It was such a simple idea that the visual model that spread through various types of media quickly became shared by millions of other children around the world. This largely crowd-sourced production process was spread on social media, and many engaged with this information because it was clear and authentic: children carrying hand-made posters asking adults to do something about their future.

By contrast, most of the ideas that dominate our current public communication are produced by industrial communication operations such as marketing and public relations firms and think tanks. For example, the market fundamentalist, or neoliberal economic model that most people on the planet continue living with today did not travel spontaneously into the world. As we will see in Chapter 3, ideas about shrinking government, and restricting collective democratic control over economic policies, came from a relatively small movement of business elites, economists, and opportunistic politicians, who developed the brilliant idea of using networks of think tanks to produce ideas suited to different political contexts. That original information production system is now named The Atlas Network and includes some 500 affiliated think tanks in over ninety countries around the world, and many more aligned political organizations.[45]

These networks of politicians, rightwing movements, think tanks, parties, and media sites often attack climate science and advocates for change. Even Greta Thunberg was attacked by politicians and media personalities around the world, from Australia, to the United States, to Germany, and beyond. They used similar talking points about her mental health and mocked the irrational fears she and her followers harbored about climate. That disinformation was politically produced and distributed by think tanks such as the Heartland Institute in the US, and affiliated media sites such as *Watts Up with That?*

By comparison, the organization of idea production among groups and citizens concerned about our current existential crises lacks anything close to the same degree of coordination. Of course, most of us would not want to engage in the degree of coordinated deception and disinformation spread by the neoliberal political economy movement. However, there are already hundreds of small think tanks and research organizations that produce high-quality, scientifically grounded information, but they are not well organized enough to produce more commonly communicated ideas and political strategies. The coming chapters identify mechanisms to improve the coordination of idea production across this range of different organizations.

Packaging Ideas

Communication scholars and practitioners often talk about how to frame messages to highlight particular information and emotions and deflect competing messages. Beyond framing, there are other aspects of packaging that affect how ideas pass through the production stage and into society. For example, we know that ideas are more likely to flow when expressed and shared through assemblages of pictures, memes, intersectional category logics, trusted sources, and diverse media formats and platforms. Such packaging delivers similar ideas to different audiences, while enabling different networks to find ways to talk to each other.

In the case of Greta Thunberg, and the millions of students sharing their alarm about the future, the packaging was simple, homemade and heartfelt. Those hand-painted signs, hopeful faces and eloquent statements added to the appeal of "generation next" calling for action from their elders. An interesting part of the packaging was the widespread adoption of Fridays as the day to leave school to raise attention to the environment. This soon gave the movement its name, *Fridays For Future*, which became a powerful focus for the identity and organization of the movement.[46]

By contrast, the packaging of neoliberal ideas used to sell market deregulation and limited government was different for citizen, business, or government audiences. The language and images aimed at individuals often appealed to the more self-centered instincts of people: images of consuming more, being free from government regulation and high taxes, and greater choice over former public goods and services such as health, education, transportation, and even water and power. Business groups were presented with the advantages of reduced regulation, lower taxes and labor costs, and reduced social and environmental responsibilities.

So many different packages and delivery methods were required to sell neoliberalism that the communication often became highly deceptive, particularly as wages began to flatten, private services failed to deliver on their promised superiority, and environmental deregulation resulted in escalating resource depletion, pollution, and waste. As popular doubts increased, political organizations and think tanks produced neatly packaged disinformation for publics on media sites and less visible briefings for elected officials and legislators. As discussed in Chapter 3, a good deal of political communication on economic, environmental, and political issues has become "weaponized" to wage deceptive information wars that could not be won with evidence or reason.

It is clear that most of us concerned about the climate crisis favor facts and reason over deception. But packaging more transparent ideas should be appealing, without sacrificing the contents or unduly restricting their travel. Even appealing packages such as a Green New Deal must have specific content directed at various networks. For example, citizens may be attracted to features involving work, leisure, health, education, or mobility. Business packages can address concerns about production, profits, taxes, and future operations in a different economy. Packages also must help organize different frames, images, and narratives so they flow across diverse networks, with enough common support to pressure politicians who announce Green new deals to make sure there is meaningful substance inside.

Networking Ideas

Thanks to digital technologies and human creativity, it does not take great resources these days to create large networks. Within six months of Greta Thunberg's remarkable solo protests in Stockholm, more than a million children in over one hundred nations had joined *Fridays For Future*, and by the end of the year, millions more had joined the global movement. While the children's movement has been effective in focusing attention by packaging familiar ideas differently, it is typical of the crowd-enabled movements discussed above in not having much capacity to coordinate detailed programs for change.

By contrast, many of the networks opposing environmental action are much more formally organized, better resourced, and have better access to media platforms to spread their ideas. Such organized ties help those networks grow and become stable and effective. As shown in Chapter 3, much of the opposition to climate action was coordinated and funded by even larger networks of organizations calling for limited government and business deregulation. And those networks in turn were supported by oil companies and other business interests that gathered at donor conferences and events organized by foundations and political organizations. Developing such effective networks involved strategic vision, starting with the many think tanks that formed local, national, and international relationships with parties, politicians, and interest organizations. Those networks grew even further with ties to trade associations such as the International Chamber of Commerce, and through connections with elite business networks such as the World Economic Forum that meets in Davos, Switzerland, each year. Those networks connecting business interests, academics, parties, and governments help explain why neoliberal political economic models, and related resistance to dealing with the climate crisis, gained such widespread political uptake over the last few decades.

The networking among organizations concerned about the environment tends to be far less developed. The idea-flow model shows how this fragmentation can be addressed by a combination of: (a) shifting the focus to more common intersectional ideas that join environment, new economy, and political reform groups, (b) changing funding strategies for those organizations so that funders promote broader cooperation around more aligned ideas; and (c) packaging ideas in more emotionally positive ways, which invite ordinary people and various stakeholder sectors to participate in the development of broadly shared popular narratives. These features of networking have worked well for the neoliberal economics movement, and for movements and parties on the radical right, and they could be adapted by advocates for more positive change, with the refreshing twist of more truthful packaging!

Political Uptake

Greta Thunberg and her millions of fellow future citizens projected a form of political influence that engaged broad attention. #FridaysForFuture presented an authentic claim to be heard and represented. Students exercised their power to leave school and assemble in public. But they had few resources, beyond their heartfelt pleas to compel those in power to think and act differently. If organizations across different issue sectors could produce, package, and network more widely shared ideas, there would be more hope to pressure politicians and parties to lead public conversations.

Political uptake can happen in various ways: incorporating ideas in party programs and agendas, promoting them in election campaigns, developing legislation and policies, and even reforming political institutions. It is important for change networks to make sure that what is taken up politically is more than just the pretty packaging. Political pressure from the streets, to elections, to political bargaining sessions needs to ensure that transformative ideas actually get into packages such as a Green New Deal, or we will repeat the history of sustainable development in which the component ideas inside the package never fit well together.

A useful comparison case is again provided by various networks promoting neoliberal economics that devoted a good deal of effort to include members of important political circles around the world. Those early adopting politicians were primed for political uptake when political opportunity presented itself with the collapse of the postwar global monetary system in the 1970s. The global economic breakdown was compounded by national failures of the formerly dominant Keynesian economic model to either explain or deal with a puzzling combination of debt, economic stagnation, and inflation. This presented an opportunity for changing economic thinking, just as rising politicians like Margaret Thatcher and Ronald Reagan were looking for new ideas to sell to parties and voters. Fast forward fifty years, and we see that the philosophy of market deregulation and related ideas of business supremacy have spread through most parties across the center-left to the center-right around the democratic world. From there, these ideas have been taken up by many social institutions, universities, and civil-society organizations.

One moral of the political uptake story is to have ideas positioned for uptake when opportunities present themselves. In today's world, there are growing signs of strain and instability in the current economic system, and in the ideas used to prop it up. The Covid-19 pandemic exposed vulnerabilities in job security and health systems in many nations. Such crises create opportunities to think differently about national values. The environmental crisis only increases those opportunities. This is an historic moment to imagine how to produce ideas differently, package and network them more effectively, and find mechanisms of power to compel parties and leaders to promote and implement them. Even if it takes existential threats such as displacement of coastal populations, escalating species extinction, or an economic crash to somehow transcend political barriers to change, it would be good to have a few well-positioned ideas about what sort of change makes sense.

History suggests, all too painfully, that there are no guarantees that good ideas will be waiting when opportunities for change appear. The question is how a better set of ideas can be developed and positioned for uptake as new opportunities arise. Fortunately, the main problem is not finding the ideas. Many good ideas are already out there, as will become clear later in the book. Currently missing are communication strategies and processes for producing, packaging, and distributing those ideas about social and environmental prosperity more widely across groups and publics, and positioning them for uptake by political parties and other institutions.

2

What's Missing in Environmental Communication?

Imagine living in societies that work better to provide health, education, housing, food, and transportation for more people, while reducing financial risk and providing more opportunities for advancement. While we are dreaming, let's add to our wish list better management of production, consumption, and wastes within environmental capacities to support both current and future economic activity. Some societies clearly do better on these things than others, but many nations today suffer from growing inequalities, shrinking opportunities, and deteriorating environments.

Despite these trends, the mantra of economic growth continues to promise illusory benefits that generally end with more wealth concentrated in the upper strata of society. That concentration of wealth generally translates into resistance from business elites and their political allies to major changes in the political and economic systems that benefit them. The failures to address growing economic problems add to both environmental and economic instability. Yet, mainstream politicians warn of the perils of doing too much too fast, playing on fears of losing jobs and familiar lifestyles to win votes. Indeed, there has been a long trend of doubling down after crises to introduce more austerity in society, while propping up markets and business sectors – something that Naomi Klein has called *The Shock Doctrine*.[1]

Although there are many voices calling for change, they are often singing in different choirs. Mobilizations on the left and right are pushing conflicting ideas. Since the great recession at the end of the first decade of this century, movements and parties on the radical right have translated popular anger and insecurity into expressions of ethnic nationalism, racial polarization, and condemnation of environmental action as threatening to traditional lifestyles. Meanwhile, progressive movements and leaders have pushed variations of Green new deals into election and policy debates.

In the wake of the Covid-19 crisis, many nations (and the world) are at political and economic crossroads between more shock doctrines that fuel reactionary politics and crony capitalism versus developing more vibrant ways of life based on new economic thinking. Whether or not new directions offering better environmental prospects emerge depends importantly on the capacity of progressive movements and their political allies to join around clear and compelling ideas about economies that work better for people and the planet. Among other things, this requires currently factionalized environmental and new economy movements to shift gears from continuing to wage narrow issue campaigns, to organizing for more fundamental economic changes. This requires recognizing the category mistakes of isolated causes, and the backwards logics of trying to fix symptoms and outputs rather than the underlying problems. These basic communication heuristics were outlined in Chapter 1. The simple proposition here is that the direction of change is often shaped by groups able to promote clear ideas and develop strong organizations to mobilize political pressure to bring those ideas into elections, party agendas, and government policies. This chapter explores the mixed record of environmental movements in these terms, from the production of smart ideas in different wings of the movement, to the lack of broadly shared strategies to communicate and act more effectively on those ideas.

Why Ideas Matter

Several generations of today's citizens have now grown up in nations that allow more of our life chances to be determined by market forces that are heralded as the arbiters of true merit. For generations that have come of age since the 1980s it may seem somehow natural to live like this. But if one goes back to the era after World War II, it becomes clear that there are other ways to organize social life around fairer distribution of economic proceeds, better health and retirement benefits, transportation systems that worked more effectively and cost less, and education systems and employment opportunities that offered more hope for advancement. The relatively higher levels of shared prosperity in Europe and North America during the 1950s and 1960s were achieved through political bargains struck in many democracies between business and labor and brokered by governments. As the coming pages show, there was also a growing environmental movement during this time that began public discussions about bringing this prosperous economy more in line with the capacities of the planet to support it. We will see what became of that discussion.

Postwar prosperity was not enjoyed by all, particularly among nations in the global south transitioning from colonialism. Corrupted governments sold natural resources and commodities to northern companies, making local populations dependent on the whims of global economic commodity cycles. But nearly everywhere, economic growth came at the expense of the environment. The industrialization of nature came overlaid with images of progress, strength and prosperity that fueled cultural insensitivities to environmental costs. It did not help that all major schools of economics "externalized" such costs from their models, because they are hard to calculate and because the natural environment appeared elastic.

Many unsettling environmental trends became evident during this era of growing prosperity in the north. Some symptoms from things like industrial pollution and growing personal automobile use were hard to miss, such as the burning smog in cities from London to Los Angeles. When concerns were raised about unhealthy environmental conditions, many nations and localities passed laws to help improve air and water quality. And when science began to detect larger patterns of industrial degradation of environments, popular books spread the word that different economic principles were available to strike a better balance between economy and environment. From the 1960s on, environmental movements of impressive size developed. Many of these networks embraced popular literatures about protecting earth systems with steady state or circular economies that struck a better balance between resources, pollution, and human industry.

Despite many gains in symptomatic relief from smog and water pollution and banning some industrial and agricultural toxics during this era, those impressive popular movements did not succeed in bringing economic systems into line with planetary capacities. While political conflicts over these issues continue to the present day, the chances for more environmentally friendly economies continue to be swept aside by the force of another set of ideas. A much smaller and less popular movement of economic and political elites advocated loosening government control of economies and allowing environmental and human fates to be determined by the interplay of markets and wealth.

We continue to live under the force of this idea system of limited government and free-market economics today, although there has been sharp criticism of neoliberal globalization on the left and, more recently, concerns about loss of national economic and cultural sovereignty from the right. Donald Trump's trade wars, and the UK decision about Brexit are just two examples of cracks in the global economic system. But few of those attacks on the economic order challenge the principle of high economic growth, and few offer plausible ideas about how to bring economies more in line with mounting evidence of environmental collapse.

This chapter and the next tell the story of these two movements that have shaped the thinking of our time. One has promoted a wide variety of ideas about protecting the environment, including many promising but still scattered economic models for rethinking prosperity within planetary boundaries. The other movement, with greater resources and better coordinated networks of proponents advanced a utopian vision of markets freed of government regulation so that individuals and enterprises might realize their full competitive potential, the planet be damned.

These two great movements have dominated a good deal of attention for the last half-century, and both have contributed to important policies that affect how we live. But the so-called neoliberal free-market regime has become far more politically dominant than the environmental movement, with the result that economic systems are clashing profoundly with the environment. The next chapter shows how the neoliberal brand of deregulation and free-market thinking achieved such dominance over more environmentally friendly economics. This chapter suggests how those concerned about the environment can develop ideas better positioned for political uptake when new opportunities arise, as they surely will. Both analyses use the idea-flow model to compare how the core ideas of these competing movements were produced, packaged, networked, and ended up with different levels of political uptake based on their relative power and influence.

The Fragmentation of Ideas in the Modern Environmental Movement

Concerns about the quality of the natural environment and its relation to human enlightenment and wellbeing have been expressed for hundreds of years. However, the modern environmental movement based on scientific evidence about the environmental impact of human economic activities can be traced to the late 1950s and early 1960s. Since that time, many millions of people around the world have developed an awareness that economies based on oil, pesticides, and other toxic chemicals, unregulated resource consumption, and unchecked wastes were harmful to people and other life forms.

An early warning came in the form of a book in 1962 by marine biologist Rachel Carson, who wrote about the life threatening dangers of pesticides and other industrial chemicals in her book *Silent Spring*.[2] Carson chronicled the pervasive uses of toxic chemicals in natural environments, resulting in the silencing of bird and wildlife populations, and even endangering the national icon, the bald eagle. She also alerted a broad public to the link between those industrial poisons and cancer in humans. The book sold some six million copies and was translated into thirty languages.

There was, as might be expected, strong pushback from the chemical industry that promoted its products as clean, modern, and enabling economic progress. There was also dissent from some in the scientific community whose work fueled industrial agriculture and other advertised advances in modern living. For example, Norman Borlaug, who would later win the Nobel Prize for his development of new food grains, dismissed Carson's concerns and credited agricultural chemicals with enabling the "Green revolution" that fed more people than previously possible. Despite the criticisms from business and agricultural science, Carson's warnings about species loss and health risks seemed visionary to many people and attracted attention around the world. Many credit Carson and her public scholarship with providing the early ideas for broadening an environmental movement beyond its then historic roots in conservation, stewardship, and preservation of natural beauty, which had a far longer tradition that ran from Henry David Thoreau's *Walden*, to Aldo Leopold's *A Sand County Almanac*, that appeared at the end of the 1940s.

Other idea streams soon appeared, including popularly accessible introductions to human systems based on scientific models predicting that resource depletion associated with unnaturally high economic growth would exhaust the life-support capacity of the finite planet. The most influential of these statements was issued in 1972 by the Club of Rome, a gathering of scientists, business elites, government officials, and representatives of civil-society organizations, which was co-founded by an Italian industrialist. One of the main activities of the club continues to be commissioning reports on various sustainability related topics such as resource depletion, new economic models, managing societal transitions, and governing our common resources.[3] The first of these reports was *The Limits to Growth*, published in 1972, which sold more than sixteen million copies (some reports are higher) in some thirty languages.[4] The report predicted global economic and civilization collapse by the mid twenty-first century if nations did not shift to economic models that better manage limited resources.

This early popular interest in the impact of human systems on the life-support capacity of the planet was further sparked by the emerging field of ecological economics, based on ideas about circular or steady state economics. The work of Herman Daly on steady state economics stands out as an early statement of ideas about how governments could balance resource consumption and wastes to assure long-term prosperity for human populations.[5] Similar thinking continues to be produced today, as in Kate Raworth's popular *Doughnut Economics*, discussed earlier, which shows what adjustments need to happen for humans to live within planetary boundaries.[6]

The spread of these early ideas in the 1960s and 1970s spurred a large international environmental movement that expanded the ranks of civil-society organizations, formed Green parties, staged protests, and successfully pushed for important policy changes to curb air pollution, protect water quality, phase out nuclear power, and set standards for automobile emissions, among many other areas. Despite such important improvements in immediate environmental quality (e.g. air, water, regulation of some toxics), the larger dream of shifting toward more sustainable economic systems was soon to become dangerously compromised.

The following discussion uses the idea-flow framework to explain how various perspectives on environmental protection spread widely around the world and continue to be expressed by the many millions calling for action today. This analysis also highlights some of the reasons why the political and economic agendas of this movement have become scattered across different issues and political strategies. Finally, we will see why the single most enduring political uptake of environmental ideas turned out to be most unfortunate. As noted in Chapter 1, the still common idea of sustainable development launched by the United Nations Commission on Environment and Development in 1987 has ultimately resulted in the subordination of more decisive environmental action to the still-dominant political agendas of economic growth and free markets. The conclusion of this chapter points to strategic political and communication shifts that may help reverse this pattern of environmental degradation by economies that are consuming their own future.

Competing Sources of Idea Production

Understanding the context in which they are produced helps explain why some ideas become influential and others do not. Before publishing *Silent Spring*, Rachel Carson had already become a bestselling nature author during her career as a marine biologist, writing several popular books about the sea. Her concern for the preservation of nature led her to become involved with environmental groups such as the Nature Conservancy and the Audubon Naturalist Society, which was famous for its beautiful coffee-table books about birds. The Audubon Society had become concerned about the impact on bird life of government and agricultural spraying programs against harmful insects, and it supported Carson because of her visibility and scientific reputation. Their mutual goal was to raise awareness about the pervasiveness of toxic chemicals and to publicize scientific findings about the hazards to wildlife. Such relationships between organizations with interests to promote and credible information sources are common in the production of ideas. For example, advertising regularly uses popular celebrities to endorse products.

Other kinds of organizations with different agendas also produced ideas that fed into different wings of the environmental movement. For example, since its founding in 1968, the Club of Rome (CoR) has gathered scientists, members of governments, businesses, and others concerned about "the future of humanity." For nearly every year since 1972, the CoR has commissioned high-profile reports on economics, environment, population, and international governance. As noted above, the most famous of these big-idea statements was *Limits to Growth* in 1972. Subsequent reports have carried evocative titles such as *Limits to Privatization*, *Bankrupting*

Nature, *The Capacity to Govern*, and *Reinventing Prosperity*.[7] These reports are circulated widely in the influence networks of club members, funders, and supporters.

Other ideas that began circulating during the 1970s focused on updating early classical thinking about economic activity and growth within limits. Many current ideas about living sustainably can be traced to nineteenth-century philosopher John Stuart Mill, who advocated what he called a stationary state economy in which wealth was not the end goal of economic activity. His reasoning was based on a combination of values and logic. On the values side, Mill argued that wealth is not intrinsically valuable; it is best understood as means to higher human ends. The pragmatism of the argument was based on the idea that while many other human values are relatively unlimited, wealth accumulation cannot be boundless due to limits on the material resources and the diminishing market value of overproduction. Mill argued that when a stable point is reached between production, resources, and human needs, economies will stabilize, and offer people opportunities to learn to value other pursuits such as art, culture, community, and self-improvement.[8]

Mill drew some of his inspiration from Adam Smith, the early pioneer of market economics who emphasized moral principles as necessary for markets to work. Smith saw that supplies of natural resources and demands of populations tended to naturally limit economic growth at different points in different nations. That point would occur when scarcity of resources or weakening demand produced diminishing returns on investments of capital and labor, as though some "hidden hand" naturally adjusted markets into stable patterns. (Among other departures from Smith's thinking, latter-day neoliberal doctrines located morality in markets, embraced growth, and largely absolved the rich from responsibilities to society.)

A contemporary update of those early ideas about economic limits was developed by Herman Daly, who pioneered the field of ecological economics and produced the idea of a steady state (sometimes called circular) economy. Unlike mainstream economics, these models included the long-term costs of resource depletion and waste disposal. They also explained how renewable resources should be managed, and how the problems of resources and wastes could be added to the costs of production and consumption.[9] Daly also helped develop the Genuine Progress Indicator which measures economic prosperity far more sensibly than GDP, as discussed in Chapter 4. These ideas continue to be produced and refined at various research centers today,[10] and have been expanded by many authors.[11]

Despite their influence in different wings of the environmental movement, these different strains of environmental thinking have never achieved overall integration. As a result, different factions of the movement are more likely to agree on sounding alarms than on promoting common and effective solutions.

Better Packaging for Alarms than Solutions

There is great potential for these different founding ideas to come together in an overarching critique of runaway economics, and the promotion of inspiring alternative models for living. Unfortunately, that has not happened, as different wings of the environmental movement have promoted different fragments of this intellectual history. For example, conservation and naturalist organizations championed ideas about life-threatening environmental toxins, but those groups were not particularly interested in changing economic systems beyond addressing sources of pollution. This may be due to the fact that organizations concerned about nature conservation were often funded by wealthy individuals with little interest in broader economic transformation. Other ideas were too complex to package in simple ways that offered clear solutions. For example, Club of Rome reports on earth systems involved models that went well beyond economic and environmental activity to include population growth, global governance, and other issues. Still other potentially important ideas have been marginalized because they lacked endorsement from mainstream academic authorities. For example, most thinking about steady state economics has been produced outside of the mainstream economic departments, think tanks, and policy centers, resulting in less recognition than given to many less-sensible but better-branded perspectives.

The challenges of integrating these different streams of ideas have left environmental activism less coherently organized and less clearly communicated than the more unified (though surely not uniform) utopian visions of the neoliberals. Many prominent environmental organizations have followed a path of promoting highly specific issues and campaigns help brand the organizations and attract particular kinds of followers and funders. One result has been a relative lack of stable cooperation aimed at generating overarching ideas and policy agendas. An indicator of this is that when the European Union began to develop "civil-society platforms" in the 1990s to better connect national NGOs with Brussels, many policy sectors such as youth, families, women, economic development, or immigration were able to form single umbrella organizations to handle their coordination. The environmentalists could not agree on forming a single coordinating organization, so their platform became the "Green Ten." The member organizations of this platform reflect the reasons why the environmental movement should be thought of as a collection of interests rather than a well-networked movement: Birdlife Europe, Climate Action Network, European Environmental Bureau, Friends of the Earth Europe, Transport and Environment, Bank Watch (financial monitoring), Nature Friends International, Health and Environment Alliance, Greenpeace European Unit, and WWF European Policy Office.[12]

Some of these organizations have origins and histories that have even caused frictions within the environmental movement. For example, consider the WWF, which began as the World Wildlife Fund in 1961 and later changed its name to World Wide Fund for Nature (although branches in the US and Canada retained the original name). WWF is often billed as the world's largest conservation organization with some five million members globally, operations in around one hundred countries, over $10 billion invested in projects since its founding, and an annual budget of nearly $350 million for just the US affiliate. However, the somewhat awkward fit between WWF and more progressive organizations began with the early founders and funders that included Prince

Bernhard of the Netherlands, the Duke of Edinburgh, and South African tobacco magnate Anton Rupert. In addition to their wealth and political conservatism, those figures had ties to the Bilderberg Group of political and business elites, who met regularly to discuss North Atlantic relations and strategies for developing European and global free-market capitalism. Prince Bernhard was born to German nobility and became a member of the Nazi Party before the war. However, after marrying the future queen Juliana of the Netherlands, he fought the Nazis for the Dutch and later the British. He also served as first chairman of the Bilderberg Group, which was named for the hotel he owned in the Netherlands where the meetings were held. He later served as the first president of WWF Europe.[13] There has been a long history of different WWF national organizations taking funding from, and occasionally honoring corporate sources with dubious environmental records. This has led to charges of "Green washing" from other environmentalists. Such divisions among environmental organizations make it all the more difficult to take next steps toward more intersectional communication that combines economic and environmental thinking.

None of this should minimize many important gains and examples of cooperation among various organizations over the years, particularly in fighting particular types of pollution, trying to save endangered species, or pressing for more renewable energy. Yet the lack of overarching economic and political vision has limited larger change initiatives. Even many moments of relative success have fallen short of meeting their transformative potential. For example, a United Nations Environmental Program audit showed that even if nations comply with their voluntary commitments to reduce CO_2 in the Paris Climate Agreement, the overall volumes are rising so fast that the agreement will fall far short (by about one third!) of its own stated goals for slowing temperature increase.[14] Once again, categorizing environmental problems in isolation from economics, and treating symptoms rather than underlying causes, have put the movement at a political disadvantage.

The power imbalances between environmental and economic interests may reinforce the tendency to produce and package ideas around relatively specific problems and solutions. Narrower issues can be packaged neatly, for example, by naming toxic chemicals, identifying their particular effects, and proposing specific solutions. And so, we continue to tell stories about how particular chemicals are killing animals or harming people, and package them with emotionally arousing images that gain public attention. Such communication is easy to grasp and attracts support from funders and publics. Focused campaigns also offer goals around which organizations can mobilize, and those campaigns have resulted in a fair number of victories. Unfortunately, those victories seldom change the underlying systems that created the problems. As a result, new versions of the same problems inevitably recur, leading to repetitions of the same political communication cycles.

In many ways, the environmental story is difficult to tell, since it covers so many aspects of life and involves so much scientific detail. By contrast, economic ideas tend to be simpler to grasp, at least in their popular versions. As we will see in the next chapter, it was far easier to tell the story of how free markets and limited government regulation would create greater freedom for individuals and more wealth for everyone, particularly when that story was packaged with endorsements from Nobel-Prize-winning economists and delivered in folksy language by trusted politicians. As it happened, however, that story turned out to be largely untrue for most people beyond its core proponents of wealthy business interests and their political allies. Many people discovered that instead of greater freedom, they experienced higher risk, uncertainty, austerity, and stress. Over time, the neoliberal project required packaging with increasing deception and disinformation, as discussed below.

As discontent with the current economic system grows, and as the Covid-19 pandemic revealed the fragility of the global economy, opportunities have opened up for positioning new economic ideas. The challenge is to find ways to better coordinate idea production when the many concerned citizens and organizations lack the processes and external incentives to find more common economic and political standpoints. Until this happens, the many different issue tribes will continue coming together in protests, calling attention to the many planetary crises, and in rallies outside the annual UN climate summits; but they will continue to lack consensus about what the core problems are, or how to address them effectively. The result is an interesting duality in which shared awareness of general problems enables impressively large protests and broad support for some eminently sensible measures such as renewable energy or auto emission standards. Yet agreement begins to fragment when it comes to how (or whether) to reorganize global economic relations, or even how to reorganize broad economic sectors such as food production, transportation, housing, private and public investment, or consumer goods production and pricing.

This duality of shared general concern tempered by specific issue divergence is reflected in two broadly different kinds of idea packaging associated with the environmental movement: *awareness packaging* focuses public attention on the big picture, while *solution packaging* breaks the movement down into hundreds of scattered issues and interest campaigns, from wildlife and nature preservation, to carbon taxes, to renewable energy, to electric cars. As noted above, these solutions operate within the existing economic and political systems that continue to generate more problems than the focus on narrow solution packages can address. There is, in short, a mismatch between success at generating levels of awareness, and the capacity of thousands of organizations and millions of active citizens to define core issues in common and work toward more transformative solutions.

Awareness Packaging. Few movements can match environmentalism in gaining the awareness of broad publics about the increasingly precarious state of the planet. Perhaps the most impressive early packaging of planetary concern involved the circulation of images of the planet taken from outer space. The early rise of the modern environmental movement coincided with the launching of space exploration, and iconic photographic images of earth taken from beyond the atmosphere. These icons drew the attention of large populations as they appeared on the covers of books, on television broadcasts, coffee mugs and T-shirts. Those early impressions of the earth as a tiny and isolated object in the vast darkness graced the covers of *The Whole Earth Catalogue*, which became popular among members of the counterculture movement of the late 1960s. Many editions of the catalogue were published by alternative living and technology pioneer Stuart Brand, who helped persuade the US National Aeronautics and Space Administration to release the images taken from various satellite missions.

Those images became part of the packaging of the idea of "spaceship earth" that had already become a meme traveling widely in society. Although various references to earth as a self-contained spaceship had appeared before in literature, the packaging of ideas and images helped the meme spread, particularly after Barbara Ward, a well-known British public intellectual, published an international bestseller titled *Spaceship Earth* in 1966. The book outlined the limited resources on the planet and the need to provide for a sustainable existence for populations both north and south. A year earlier, Adlai Stevenson, a friend of Ward and then US Ambassador to the United Nations, delivered a speech using the same idea: "We travel together, passengers on a little spaceship, dependent on its vulnerable reserves of air and soil, all committed for our safety to its security and peace ... we cannot maintain it half fortunate, half miserable, half confident, half despairing ... No craft, no crew can travel safely with such contradictions. On their resolution depends the survival of us all."[15]

Around the same time, prominent economist Kenneth Boulding (who served as environmental advisor to US President John F. Kennedy) wrote a widely circulated paper called "The Economics of the Coming Spaceship Earth," which pointed out the need for a "cyclical economic system" to better balance resource limits, waste processing, and population needs.[16] Images of life on a limited and precious planet continue to this day, packaged in all manner of ways from the annual celebrations of Earth Day since 1970, to more recent protesters waving hand-made drawings of earth packaged around slogans such as "There is No Planet B."

Every generation for the last half century has found ways to direct attention to the growing crisis. As noted earlier, world attention has been focused in this century by the calls of the children in the Fridays for Future movement. Within six months of Greta Thunberg's vigil in front of the Swedish Parliament in August 2018, a strike of some 1.4 million children took place in 112 countries. During the week of those protests, Google worldwide search trends on "climate change" peaked far above their levels over the past year, and stayed at a higher level, corresponding to a huge spike in searches for Greta Thunberg.[17]

From images of the lonely planet in space, to polar bears stranded on shrinking ice floes, to the iconic face of Greta Thunberg, there is no shortage of effective attention-getting memes. However, the question becomes: What do we do, now that we have your attention? It is here that the solution packages often fall short of addressing the nature and magnitude of the underlying problems.

Solution Packaging. Unfortunately the attention-getting images of the whole earth as fragile and at risk are not matched by the proliferation of small, fragmentary solutions packaged and distributed by environmental advocates. Until environmental problems are categorized and packaged to include needed economic and political changes, the number of narrowly defined environmental problems will continue to grow, and the solution packages will be far too small. Even a short list of current environmental problem categories suggests thousands of needed solutions awaiting inside each one: biodiversity loss and species extinction; declining water quality and availability; myriad forms of pollution from industrial chemicals; toxic byproducts of industrial animal farming; increasing urbanization and population concentration and related stresses on land, sanitation and health; production and transportation systems feeding global consumerism; and continued growth of fossil fuel usage, even as more renewables come on line. And, of course, there is carbon-dioxide-related climate change, which feeds in and out of many of these problems.

And every year the list grows. The United Nations provides annual updates on emerging new categories of problems. For example, the UN emerging issues list for 2018–2019 included: the release of synthetic and bioengineered technologies into nature, disconnection of formerly integrated ecosystems due to deforestation, damming rivers and other activities; and the startling rate of permafrost thaw causing release of greenhouse gases and other dormant risks.[18] Each of these categories includes dozens of more specific problems for which there are separate scientific discussions and political struggles over what the solutions might look like. To the extent that publics are even aware of any of these thousands of issues, it is largely because their packaging is focused, emotionally arousing, and promises clear solutions.

As a result of the proliferation of narrow issues and causes, our political communication space is occupied with bite-sized packaging of problems and solutions vying for public and political attention. As noted earlier, the logical dilemma is that even when victories occur, new problems soon replace the old ones. For example, it is clear that the work of Rachel Carson and many others limited use of the bug killer DDT (dichloro-diphenyl-trichloroethane). That deadly chemical builds up in environments, in animal tissues and travels up the food chain, endangering birds and other species, including humans. DDT was widely used on crops and in households, and it was linked to great collateral damage in other species including humans. What is less well known is that even after being banned in the US and other northern nations, DDT use continued in the global south where it was deemed the most cost-effective way to kill the mosquitoes that infect millions of people with malaria every year. The pricing of replacement chemicals deemed safer was too high for poor countries or world health programs to afford. Even though DDT-resistant mosquitoes produced rebounds in malaria, the chemical continues to be used in some areas.

Meanwhile, back in the north, new chemical threats soon came along because outlawing DDT did nothing to change the underlying partnership between chemical companies and industrial agriculture, which continues to generate new versions of the same problems. Unfortunately, activists often continue to fight the old battles over again using the same idea packaging. For example, chemical companies such as Dow, DuPont, or Monsanto (later purchased by German chemical giant Bayer) shifted to developing genetically modified plants that resist pests and are tolerant to powerful herbicides that kill invasive weeds. The invention of glyphosates (popularized under the brand name Roundup by Monsanto) enabled chemical companies to monopolize both genetically engineered crop seeds, and the compatible chemicals that help them grow. In what seems like a replay of the Silent Spring story of DDT, research has found that Roundup concentrates in soil, causes birth defects in animals, and has become part of many foods eaten by large human populations. Roundup/glyphosate produces plant-threatening bacterial diseases that endanger natural seed stocks. Such frightening developments actually threaten more natural methods of farming.

Despite these recurring cycles of worsening problems, twenty-first-century anti-Roundup campaigns are much the same as the anti-DDT crusades of the last century. One YouTube video is subtitled: "Rachel Carson We Need You Again." The sponsoring organizations just for that video include: Pesticide Action Network, North America; Moms Across America; Moms for Sustainability; Environmental Working Group; and Slow Food USA; and viewers are referred to a dozen more allied NGOs and public information organizations.[19] As with DDT, there have been some clear victories, but the overall results have been less than decisive. Some nations have now banned the herbicide for farm and home use. Monsanto (and new owner Bayer) has been sued for billions for hiding evidence that its products caused cancer. And other research suggests that glyphosates may contribute to the death of honeybee populations, raising new categories of problems with few clear solutions. At the time of this writing, the US Environmental Protection Agency of the Trump administration declared Roundup safe.

Continuing battles over specific solutions today seem like echoes from the past, but there is an important difference. The failure to tackle underlying causes means that the systems producing the problems have grown more complex and entrenched. In the case of genetically modified seeds that are resistant to herbicides and pesticides, the process has not only produced more dangerous chemicals, but enabled corporations to patent and own important parts of our food supplies.[20]

Although logic might suggest it is time to change how we think about problems and solutions (stay tuned for Chapter

5), it is understandable why the formulas for most bite-sized Problem Solution Packages (PSPs) remain the same, and why they generally fail to change the game:

- PSPs fit the missions of sponsoring organizations, yet their narrowness makes it difficult to assemble larger coalitions of organizations across different issue categories
- PSPs engage the emotions of supporting publics, but fail to present larger visions of underlying problems
- PSPs fit within narrow governmental policy processes, often without disrupting larger political-business relationships
- PSPs result in clear wins or losses for environmental organizations within manageable time and resource budgets, yet small victories do not add up to winning the overall objective of stopping ecological collapse.

Perhaps most frustrating of all, these failures of PSPs to tackle deeper underlying causes often result in the emergence of new versions of the same old problems. Recall these characteristics from the partnership between Rachel Carson and the Audubon Society involving the packaging of pesticide poisoning with images of lost wildlife such as songbirds, and the rise of cancer in human populations. That packaging ticked all the characteristics of PSPs outlined above, while avoiding the root causes of the problem. As a result, environmentalists continue fighting the same battles over different generations of toxic chemicals to this day.

One can argue in defense of continuing the PSP communication logic that more fundamental challenges to alliances between politicians, big farming and chemical companies will never succeed. But stronger coordination of movements in other cases such as women's suffrage, labor, or civil rights, has overcome similarly entrenched opposition. Part of the challenge facing more coordinated and intersectional idea production involves built-in divisions among different branches of environmental activism. For example, many supporters of Carson and the DDT campaign, and continuing in this tradition today, were interested in nature conservancy or health issues, but would stop short of challenging industrial agriculture or the economic system itself.

Even more radical organizations like Greenpeace often run self-limiting communication campaigns, as in the iconic campaigns using endearing animals such as polar bears, walruses, or seals adrift in seas of melting ice. Variations on these campaigns include the sad polar bears used to pressure Coca Cola (long associated with cute cartoon polar bears as part of its image) to change its use of environmentally dangerous refrigerant gases, which it finally did. A return engagement of critters in Greenpeace campaigns again targeted Coca Cola, this time pointing to the corporate giant's enormous production of throw-away plastics that clog the oceans and endanger wildlife. Such problem-solution-packages are brilliant at a certain level, since they are bite-sized, easy to relate to and formulaic, with easily repeatable packages of elements: "polar bear (or fill in your favorite threatened species here) + specific targeted message + particular recommended solution." Unfortunately, these formulas do not enable the kind of networking around broader ideas that might add up to transformative solutions.

The Weak Networking of Environmental Ideas

While many PSP-type communication campaigns have met with success in terms of their self-defined goals, they can also reinforce organizational separation, and make broader networking difficult. For example, consider the relationship between the WWF, introduced earlier, and the polar bears. Like other organizations, WWF has used polar bears to package campaigns, including raising millions from a co-sponsored campaign with Coca Cola to develop sustainability programs for endangered polar bears in the Arctic.

After such successes, it may have been awkward to learn that, technically, the polar bear was not an "endangered" species, just a "vulnerable" one. Many other environmental organizations became concerned that packaging polar bears in endangered-species campaigns distracted public attention and political focus from far more complex ecological issues in the Arctic region. At a conference of some 400 environmental stakeholders held inside the Arctic Circle in 2018, WWF announced that it was working on a different communication strategy to try to help people understand more complex realities of climate change and impacts on all forms of life – including humans – in such fragile regions of earth. But that re-packaging would not be easy. Of the 700,000 visitors to the WWF Arctic program website the previous year, nearly two thirds were only interested in information about the polar bears.[21] Stay tuned to see if WWF packaging of Arctic issues changes, or whether it will help broader networks of organizations share more common messages and political strategies.

In these and other ways, change-oriented networks are variously limited by issue focus, organizational identity, relationships to business and government, and by funding constraints and follower interests. In addition, finding the right kinds of network partners is crucial. While networking with business can be highly desirable under the right conditions, it is important to think about goals and consequences. For example, WWF has partnered with Coca Cola in projects to preserve fresh water, but such issue-specific networking can limit venturing deeper into the realm of economic change.

Despite the richness of the ideas described earlier in the chapter, and despite growing severity of environmental disruptions, some of the most prominent environmental organizations have resisted organizing more coordinated networks to develop a clear set of economic and political ideas that can be packaged to address the sources of planetary problems. And so, conservationists still tend to rally around particular threats to life and focus on specific remedies such as removing toxic chemicals or reducing plastics. Meanwhile, operating in different networks, ecological economists continue to develop good ideas, but have had little uptake from the many other environmental organizations that do not see economic change as central to their missions. Another of the early idea streams that has generally stayed in its own lane are the systems approaches following the tradition of the Club of Rome. Although most systems thinking could be connected fairly easily to ecological economics, much of it remains abstract, hard to package, and even harder to share, with most organizations focused more on immediate threats and solutions.

Even though these different organizations and separate idea streams share a concern for the environment and the security of life, the potential for more focused networks continues to fragment into many different issues and policy campaigns. As Anthony Giddens pointed out in his book *The Politics of Climate Change*, "there is no Green movement – rather there is a diverse range of positions, perspectives, and recipes for action."[22] Giddens also wrote a screed called "We Should Ditch the Green Movement," in which he recommended "taking the issue of climate change out of the hands of the environmentalists" because they lack both an economic program and the political coherence required to help citizens and politicians see how to create different living arrangements to address the crisis.[23] In surveying these fractured networks in Germany, one environmental historian lamented: "How can one write an environmental history of Green Germany when bird lovers clash with renewable energy enthusiasts over wind power, when ecofarming is under threat from the quest for biofuels, and when the burgeoning climate-change movement is viewed with deep suspicion among advocates of biodiversity?"[24]

In recent years, some organizations have called for more cross-sectional networking, particularly between economic justice and environmental groups. However, a network mapping project that I ran for several years showed little growth in interconnections among new economics and environmental organizations in the US or in Europe. There was not even much network growth within the alternative economics sector. For example, several years of monitoring online linking among groups in the so-called "degrowth" movement in Europe shows many scattered organizations, with lots of local level activity, but not much change in the size or coherence of the overall networks, and few connections to established environmental networks. That is unfortunate, considering that the basic ideas of living in healthier societies in better balance with nature have the potential for broad appeal. Despite these and many other good ideas circulating in degrowth circles, packaging them with the intentionally shocking name "degrowth" seems a sure way to limit their growth.

The Limited Political Uptake of Real Solutions

One mark of strong movements with coherent idea networks is that they are better able to forge alliances with political parties. Giddens and others have argued that European Green parties seldom get the share of votes that they should, given the growing public awareness and concern about environmental issues. This problem is not just due to the relative weakness of movement coordination, it is also the result of Green parties distancing themselves from their early movement origins. As a result, in Germany, the Greens have moved into government in various states and localities with the Christian Democrats and the Free Democratic (liberal) Party, further alienating many of their former movement supporters. This trend may be changing, as both the Greens in Germany and at the EU level have begun to talk about a Green New Deal that better integrates economic and environmental policies. Perhaps this shift will continue, with the result that both party and movement will find each other again, with the help of voters. Following the surge of a Green coalition in the European Union elections of 2019, the German Greens for the first time registered higher public approval ratings than either of the traditionally dominant parties, the fading Christian Democrats and Social Democrats.

Until better networking around more transformative ideas produces political implementation of new economic agendas, both the networking and political uptake of environmental activism are likely to remain issue specific. For example, the conservationist wing of the environmental movement has helped focus attention on programs to protect vulnerable and endangered species. Organizations such as the Nature Conservancy, WWF, Natural Resources Defense Fund, Sierra Club, The Audubon Society, The Royal Society for the Protection of Birds, and Oceana, among many others, have also helped preserve vast areas of temperate and tropical rainforests, and drawn attention to, and helped protect endangered marine environments.[25]

A different area that can be regarded as having similar issue-specific political success is the fight for clean air. Large numbers of organizations, including some conservancy groups, have joined forces over many decades in fighting for better air quality. Air pollution is among the leading causes – and, in many places, the leading cause – of premature death and severe health problems in humans.[26] These threats continue, despite the many political victories dating well back into the last century to clean up smog, and reduce dozens of deadly particulates from vehicles, factories, and agriculture. Among the many organizations fighting for clean air today are the Sierra Club, the Union of Concerned Scientists, the Clean Air Task Force, Earth Justice (a legal support non-profit), and the German Sustainable Transport Association, just to name a few. As with so many fights, focusing solutions on the output end seldom stems the growth of underlying sources of the problem. For example, producing cleaner vehicles helps, but as long as numbers of vehicles continue to rise, the problem grows in defiance of the victories. Even electric cars require charging, and most of the power for that comes from fossil fuels. Then there is the issue of what to do with the old batteries. And so, the cascade of small problems goes on.

The lack of high-level networking and political uptake at the intersection of economic, environmental, and political ideas means that the best efforts of environmental organizations and protesters have proved poor matches for opposing business interests and political allies that dominate government in most nations. With the help of economists, think tanks, and strategic communication practitioners, those political interests effectively limit the capacities of governments to manage economies in the public or environmental interest, beyond trying to contain crises.

In the face of such a dominant idea regime, it may seem little wonder that environmentalists are at a disadvantage. But the lack of well-packaged and broadly networked ecological economic alternatives has surely not helped. To make matters worse, what many consider to be the greatest political triumph of the intersection of environmental and economic ideas – sustainable development – has turned out to be environmentalism's greatest institutionalized defeat.

The Pitfalls of Sustainable Development

As noted in Chapter 1, the idea of sustainable development swept the world after 1987 when the United Nations World Commission on Environment and the Future issued a report that was subtitled "Our Common Future."[27] The report also became known as the Brundtland report, in recognition of former Norwegian Prime Minister Gro Harlem Brundtland, who chaired the UN commission. A book version of the report titled *Our Common Future* was also published in 1987 by Oxford University Press. The report and book popularized the already emerging idea of "sustainable development," which promised the almost magical possibility that poorer nations could continue to develop (i.e. economies would grow, and societies prosper) somehow in balance with nature.

This idea of sustainable development soon took off globally, with many highly developed nations launching sustainable development agencies and commissions. For many public officials, the idea offered what seemed like a perfect compromise between expansion of the global neoliberal economic regime and growing public concerns about environmental degradation. The concept rocketed into popular imagination as the phrase far and away most commonly associated with the word sustainable in books in the English language after 1987. Note the steep rise of references to the idea immediately following the publication of the UN report and the book. Figure 2.1 shows the most common word pairs with "sustainable" in a database of some eight million books scanned in a Google project that covered works published between 1500 and 2008. While it is not possible to say that the books were randomly selected, the English corpus is the largest, containing some 350 billion words.[28] There is no reason to think that the word associations (known as Ngrams) in such a large corpus of books should be biased for or against any particular co-occurrences with the term "sustainable." The 2-grams (pairs) in Figure 2.1 clearly show that the idea of sustainable development swept the literature very quickly after it appeared.

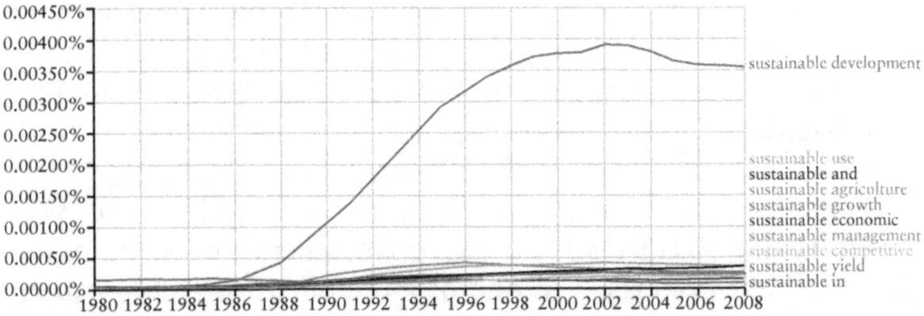

Figure 2.1 The growth of the idea of sustainable development in books published in English following the publication of *Our Common Future* in 1987. Source: Google Ngram.

Beyond its important nod to the fates of developing nations in the global south, the idea of sustainable development was less a forward-looking idea than a summary term for the decades of public pressure and political attention to relatively specific environmental issues. For example, the UK passed a Clean Air Act in 1956, and the US followed with its landmark Clean Air Act in 1963. The US Environmental Protection Agency was established in 1970 during the Republican presidency of Richard Nixon. The idea of protecting the environment gained broad international recognition when more than thirty European nations signed a cooperation agreement in 1979 to curb air pollution, which was causing acid rain that was killing forests and life in European lakes. The idea had even gained popular recognition as a core human value following a landmark UN Conference on the Human Environment held in Stockholm in 1972. That gathering established the idea of extending human rights to include healthy environments. And various nations in the UN had issued calls to help postcolonial nations end continued resource and labor exploitation in order to have economic growth with stable environments.[29]

Even though the mix of social development, economic growth, and environmental sustainability has proved elusive for more than three decades since becoming the leading economy-friendly environmental idea, it has remained attractive politically. Many nations, both north and south, created departments or agencies for sustainable development.

And the UN 2015 edition of the Sustainable Development Goals (SDGs) met with continuing enthusiasm. The Green Party of Ireland hailed the SDGs: "The UN Sustainable Development Goals are a Manifesto for the Future of both the Global North and South."[30]

The German Council for Sustainable Development was created in 2001 to advise the government on sustainable development policies.[31] In one of its publications, the council looked back to 1987 and ahead to 2030, the target for practical implementation of the UN 2015 SDGs. Citing the Brundtland report, the German Council published a *German Almanac of Sustainability* that defined sustainable development as: "… development that meets the needs of the present without compromising the ability of future generations to meet their own needs … In essence, sustainable development is a process of change in which the exploitation of resources, the direction of investments, the orientation of technological development and institutional change are all in harmony and enhance current and future potential to meet human needs and aspirations."[32] A foreword by the German foreign minister affirmed that the SDGs were pillars of national policy both domestic and foreign. The inspiring language in the report goes on to outline bold goals and a set of processes to guide a German energy transition and help lead the global south toward a better future. In the brief section on changing the economy, the report notes that at present Germany consumes resources at a pace that would require 3.1 planets to support (behind world leaders Australia at 5.4 planets, US at 4.8, and Switzerland, South Korea, and Russia all at 3.3). However, the hope is that this might be reined in closer to consuming just one planet with the combination of better energy efficiency and less exploitive trading relations with the global south.[33] While aspirational and almost magical, the report offers only marginal adjustments to try to help us all live within one planet. At least it reflects the gradual shift in attention to intersectional environmental and economic thinking.

Recall the analysis from Chapter 1, showing that meeting the SDGs is impossible because the social goals of health, education, and good jobs require unrealistic growth levels, yet even more modest growth will damage the environment.

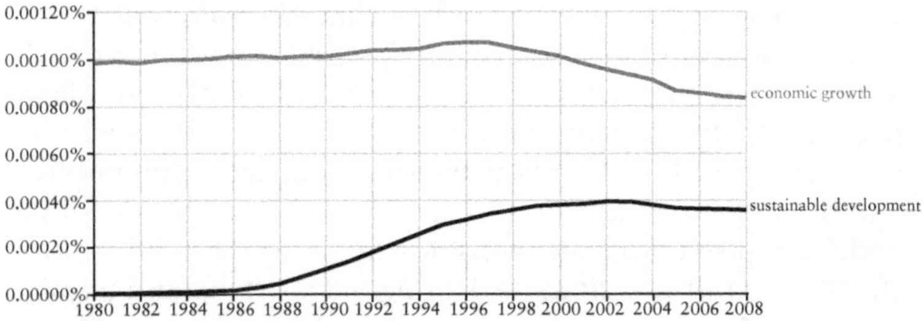

Figure 2.2 Volumes of references to "economic growth" and "sustainable development" in books published in English between 1980 and 2008. Source: Google Ngram.

Indeed, even the United Nations can point to only a few small-scale heartwarming projects to illustrate accomplishments: the use of biofuels on a family farm in Tunisia, the quest for energy autonomy and food self-sufficiency in a hamlet of 600 people in France, or a project to adopt and save olive trees in a dying region of Spain.[34] While these are charming examples, there is little evidence that sustainable development has achieved the kind of policy success needed to create anything approaching true balance between its two competing ideas. However, the idea has been highly successful as a classic example of what Murray Edelman from Chapter 1 termed "words that succeed and policies that fail."

The most damning feature of the idea of sustainable development is that it invites tradeoffs between economy and environment, rather than finding a communication format that makes them inseparable. As a result, Figure 2.2 shows that economic growth has remained the far more important concept in the popular literary imagination. As currently defined and packaged, economic growth and environmental protection seem irreconcilable on a grand scale. Economic considerations typically trump more decisive environmental measures.

While it is good to have noble goals, their realization will continue to be blocked by the current economic regime until a more plausible vision of ecological economics becomes widely shared and advocated. All of this suggests that coordinated efforts must begin to develop ideas that offer alternatives to the current regime of largely unregulated economic growth at the expense of environmental health and capacity of many species to thrive. It is time for environmental communication to become far better organized and politically competitive with the currently failing set of economic ideas. The idea-flow model can provide a framework for thinking about how more effective idea production, packaging, networking and uptake can work. A set of specific strategies and guidelines is offered in Chapter 5. First, it is helpful to look at how the idea-flow process worked in constructing the very destructive set of economic and political ideas with which we continue to live.

3

Economy vs. Environment: Selling Predatory Economics

The current global economic regime has turned into a perfect storm battering an already fragile environment. Simply switching to cleaner energy will not be enough to dislodge the underlying predatory economic logic. Meaningful gains from "clean energy" transitions are unlikely to happen without different political regulations and policies guiding a transition in modes of production, transportation, consumption, and management of the related byproducts. This chapter explores three of the converging factors that limit the capacity of many citizens, politicians, and business elites to imagine and enact such needed economic changes: the myth of growth, the myth of free markets, and the resulting political power of business to limit change.

The first economic challenge to planetary life is the popular belief that economies can and should be made to grow – the more, the better. Of course, many economists caution that reckless growth should be avoided, but the recent history of speculation in housing markets, debt crises, and unrealistic growth levels projected in the United Nations sustainable development goals, all reflect continuing public and institutional commitment to an idea that has received political uptake around the world. As described in the last chapter, growth has trumped sustainability to the point that in these times, economic stagnation offers the best prospects for environmental repair.

The daily business news is largely a cheerleading squad for rising corporate profits and stock market rallies. Particularly in the US, companies that fail to grow their profits, even over the last quarterly report, typically lose value for investors. There have been few tax incentives for companies to expand their stakeholder value portfolios beyond profits for executives and investors. However, in recent years there are signs of companies developing greater responsibility to other stakeholders, including workers, communities, and nature. Public policy can help expand and reward such moves.

Several decades after the myth of growth became institutionalized, *a second great economic myth* swept the world in the closing decades of the last century: the faith that free markets with minimal government regulation were required to unleash human enterprise, creativity, and of course, growth. This development was based on a utopian vision backed by little empirical evidence and sold through a well-organized and funded international movement of academic, business, and political elites. There are many national variants, with think tanks, parties, and business associations promoting the ideas of free markets, low taxes, limited government, private solutions for public problems, free movement of capital, tax havens, and limited responsibility of business and wealthy individuals to society, workers, or environment.

This philosophy is often termed neoliberalism. It is a revisioning, and in many ways a distortion, of the ideas of liberal moral philosopher and first economist Adam Smith, with a nod to the private property rights thinking of the earlier liberal political philosopher John Locke. However, one suspects that Professor Smith would be shocked at the perversion of many of his ideas about the moral basis of a market economy and the responsibilities of its winners to society. In recent times, neoliberalism has become a nasty epithet hurled by the left at the takeover of government by business interests and the resulting imposition of austerity and inequality. But those attempts to identify the causes of our current economic, political, and environmental discontents are largely lost on the general public. The labeling of the left has gained little traction, in part, because most of the actors involved in spreading the small government, free-market doctrines generally resist self-labeling. They point to their work as simply the natural order of things. In some cases, cloudier terms such as libertarianism have been adopted by those who embrace the personal freedoms that come from great wealth, unencumbered by limits or responsibilities. As they say, it is good to be rich.

A third element of the perfect economic storm buffeting the planet is the growing imbalance of power between business interests freed from government checks, and the diminished power of civil society – those citizen organizations, movements, and political parties that once held more sway over the regulation and distribution of economies. The growth of business power in society and politics has compromised democratic governance, resulting in increasing political and economic inequality, austerity, and social insecurity. This tilt of political economy has bent political parties and governments in democracies to its will, rendering politicians unable to offer much to voters beyond hype, spin, and disinformation. As noted earlier, this is the condition that Colin Crouch described as post-democracy. And post-democracy is a form of governance ill equipped to address our environmental crises.

Each of these aspects of the clash between economy, politics, and environment has its own story, but those stories have become entwined and often held together by disinformation and propaganda. The tangled web of communication supporting different versions of these problems varies from one country to another. For the purposes of simplicity, this chapter outlines the general political communication strategies that set these forces in motion, and points to lessons that can be learned by movements seeking better alignment of ideas about democratic reform, economic justice, and environmental protection.

And now, here comes the good news: economic and political regimes may seem fixed and unyielding, and even somehow natural, but it is good to remember that this failing system was socially and politically constructed. Moreover, it is relatively recent in origin and was built through intentional communication and organization processes. This means that this predatory form of capitalism is not a natural state of existence, but an imagined, constructed, and contested collection of national variations. Understanding how this political economy project developed may help those seeking change find more effective communication and organizational practices to put us on a better path. The following sections address the three dominant features of this predatory political economy.

The Idea of Endless Growth

Few ideas have swept the world with such acceptance as the belief that economic growth is something that can be engineered, managed, and used to develop better ways of life for growing populations. Most of the economists and politicians who have presided over this growth worship seldom utter the dirty secret that they are borrowing heedlessly against the future. It turns out that the growth bug is an historical aberration, and one that did not really hold much fascination until the idea of measuring, comparing, and artificially stimulating what has become known as "the gross domestic product" came into vogue in the 1930s. Perhaps it is time for this odd economic fashion to be replaced by more sensible models that support a good life on the basis of more sustainable principles and measures.

Classical economics stemming from the ideas of Adam Smith regarded growth not as the goal of an economy, but as something that naturally occurred or did not occur within limits of resources, population size, consumption habits, and methods of production and exchange. This was in keeping with early thinking that resources were limited, and that economic and human activities, including increases in wealth and population, were also limited by the natural environment. These ideas about growth and limits were developed more fully by the Reverend Thomas Malthus, who followed Smith with ideas that species populations always grew faster than environmental resources, and regularly crashed in natural cycles. This thinking was later adopted by those who regarded population control as essential to human prosperity. The simplistic logic of population vs. environment neatly renders government and economy invisible and has also led to some rather uncharitable positions against charity and government welfare as mechanisms that unnaturally support overpopulation and dependency. Refrains on the population thesis have been echoed ever since, from Paul Ehrlich's bestseller of the late 1960s *The Population Bomb*, to a more recent cameo appearance in Michael Moore's production, *Planet of the Humans*. And for the last fifty years, neoliberals have pressed to cut back on public welfare as an enabler for those unable to fend for themselves in competitive market societies. The Covid-19 pandemic even triggered calls for saving economies by letting weak members of societal "herds" die off so that the strong would survive and markets would thrive.

An alternative line of thinking to the natural limits to growth, whether in populations or economies, emerged in the twentieth century with the convergence of several factors that enabled economists and their political clients to believe that they could manage national economies. A number of developments made it possible to imagine buffering natural growth and crash cycles. The spread of central banking systems (long established in Sweden, England, and France, but late arriving in Switzerland, Italy, Japan, and America) enabled greater degrees of management over money supplies, credit rates, currency valuation, and inflation. Above all, the development of scientific models and measurements for complex economic systems provided tools for managing growth and crashes. Most important of these models is the still reigning measurement kit for the overall performance of economies, the Gross Domestic Product (GDP).

At the center of these new ideas about managing economic growth was a grand economic theory that reigned over economic policy around the developed world from the Great Depression of the 1930s until the 1970s, when another economic meltdown ushered in many variants of neoliberalism. Thanks to a global economic crash of 1929–1930 that caused the Great Depression, something of a political and economic paradigm shift generated enthusiasm for the ideas of British economist John Maynard Keynes, who showed how governments could (and should) manage economies. Using a mix of central banking and government spending, and assessing what was working by measuring GDP, stagnant economies could be stimulated with growth as the goal.

The future of growth was secured by Simon Kuznets who developed his measures of GDP during the same time that Keynesianism became the leading policy antidote for an economic crisis that proved unresponsive to natural market corrections. A key idea was that since governments could manage the distribution of the GDP through taxes, transfers, and outright ownership of assets, the rising tide of growth would lift all boats. (Recall James Galbraith's observation from the introduction that growth today mainly lifts all yachts.) The theory of managed growth worked well for governments dealing with the challenges of Great Depression and World War II. As these ideas were embraced by governments and political institutions, growth soon became a widespread cultural indicator for prosperity.

The convergence of Keynesian economic theory, central banking authorities, and the capacity to measure complex economies helped move the idea of growth from an incidental aspect of economic activity to a primary goal. When the political and economic institutions of the world system were restructured by the victorious democratic powers after World War II, supplies of natural resources appeared unlimited. Growing middle classes were tempted by an expanding array of consumer desires, aided by that stepchild of PR, advertising. All of this made voters receptive to politicians who promised economic growth. To this day, growth continues to be widely advertised as good for all.

One suspects that Adam Smith and the Reverend Malthus would be shocked at the folly of their successors who latched onto ideas about artificially stimulating growth with little regard for environmental limits. Kuznets, who won a Nobel Prize for his work, warned that his measure of growth was not a measure of prosperity or wellbeing, since all kinds of production and consumption, good and bad, were included in the size of an economy. Kuznets argued that measuring the size of all economic activity did not reveal anything about the qualities of things being produced or the equity with which they were distributed. He wanted his model to be tailored to assess whether economies provided social wellbeing. Although he argued against measuring economic activities with little social value, such as military spending or financial speculation, his wishes were defeated by politicians and business-minded economists who saw the role of the economy differently.

Beyond the realm of economics, the myth that growth is good has emerged in other areas of society including agriculture, where growing crops faster, bigger, and more quickly was deemed a good idea as well. In less-developed areas where nature presented real limits to even modest dreams of prosperity, chemical technologies brought on the "Green Revolution" that made it possible to feed more people than local conditions could support. It is ironic that Norman Borlaug, who won a Nobel Prize for his work on increasing food supplies in poor areas, issued warnings that unnatural growth in populations would result from the capacity to expand food production. The population growth, in turn, would create demands for more artificially engineered food supplies. As discussed in Chapter 2, the push for higher-yield agriculture also led to more rapid environmental degradation due to the introduction of toxics in soil, air, water, and food itself. Although he was concerned about population growth, Borlaug dismissed many of these environmental concerns.

Like many other moments in human history when warnings should have been heeded, concerns about economic growth were swept away by the tide of optimism that new ideas and technologies would solve any problems. And so, the stage was set for the immodestly titled conference for "A New World Order" held at Bretton Woods, New Hampshire, in 1944. A compromise was struck between the US Treasury Secretary White, who was concerned about price and trade stability, and Keynes, whose blueprint mainly focused on growth. The impressive plan resulted in 44 allied nations signing a treaty for a global monetary system to promote stable trade and economic development.

This system was to be regulated by an International Monetary Fund that monitored loans and payments, with currencies tied to a fixed price of gold. This effectively put the US dollar as the world standard, backed by the large gold reserves in Fort Knox. The centerpiece of this system was a story about eternal prosperity built upon unlimited natural resources. The US Secretary of State Henry Morgenthau outlined this vision of "a dynamic world economy where people in all countries could realize their inherent potentials under peaceful conditions, and to an increasing degree enjoy material welfare on earth with unlimited natural resources."[1] As historian Eva Friman concluded, the story of modern society became one of progress defined by growth, to the great peril of nature: "In the name of progress or development, which is closely associated with economic growth, modern society strives towards increased modification and control of nature. Such a view of nature is only possible with a separation of culture from nature. In separating culture from nature, modern society seems to run the risk of destroying the very basis of the progress it desires."[2]

During the postwar era, Keynesian economic policies continued to mix government regulation of business and labor markets, with tax policies that favored economic security and wellbeing for growing middle classes. The strength of labor movements, unions, and related parties balanced the power of business. Growing consumer societies enjoyed access to housing, cars, televisions, fashion, food, travel, education, and health care. As economies grew, the idea of government management and distribution of that growth was widely, though not universally, accepted. The capacity of mere mortals to model and intervene in something as large and chaotic as national and global economies was novel and seemed almost miraculous.

Unfortunately, that economic system had barely begun to function when it ran into too much complexity during the 1960s, which was a turbulent era on many fronts. Following the impressive but expensive reconstruction of Europe and Japan after World War II, and the booming optimism of the growing American economy in the 1950s, the 1960s saw Kennedy and Johnson administrations launch ambitious social welfare, education, and poverty relief programs at home. The government debt load grew even more severe, as the treasury also financed a long and expensive war in Vietnam. The rise of stronger economies in Japan, Germany, and France created threatening competition in currency and gold markets. As a result, the US ran massive balance of payments deficits, and there were far more dollars in circulation than could be redeemed at the fixed rate of gold. Speculation in gold ran up the open market value far beyond the agreed price of $35 per ounce. Unable to meet the terms of the Bretton Woods agreement, President Richard Nixon took the dollar off the gold standard in 1971. While that move eased the immediate economic pain, it rocked the world monetary system, and failed to relieve the debilitating domestic "stagflation" (simultaneous stagnation and inflation) that defied Keynesian logic.

Meanwhile, in the UK the British pound was taking a battering. British economic policy reflected a set of contradictions that included trying to keep the value of the currency high to encourage domestic industrial production, while suffering large trade deficits due to the unattractiveness of high priced, low quality British products such as cars. The economy plunged into recession and rising unemployment. The Labour government of Harold Wilson devalued the pound, and later Labour governments in the 1970s eventually turned to the IMF for loans, which were delivered on harsh terms. The IMF had lost much of its original mission when the Bretton Woods system collapsed following the US withdrawal from the currency agreement, but quickly transitioned to a strict disciplinary force administering shock treatments to sick economies. The British economy in the 1970s was the first recipient of what Naomi Klein later called the "shock doctrine," as discussed in more detail in the next chapter.

Adding to these pressures, the Organization of Petroleum Exporting Countries (OPEC) reacted sharply to Western support for Israel against the Arab coalition that launched the Yom Kippur War in 1973. Prior to that, OPEC had been a rather docile organization that kept the rulers of oil states very wealthy and offered cheap oil to the West. The oil cartel discovered its geopolitical might by punishing America and its allies with soaring oil prices during the decade. The oil crisis added to the already severe economic woes. Inflation rose to over 20 percent in the UK, and in both the US and UK, unemployment reached alarming levels, stock markets fell, interest rates for loans and capital expenditures rose, and growth stalled.

That mix of conditions failed to respond to the conventional Keynesian measures that were thought to stimulate economies. The apparent exhaustion of Keynesian economics produced demand for new ideas. Opportunistic politicians, including Margaret Thatcher in the UK and Ronald Reagan in the US, quickly latched onto a set of ideas that had been positioned for political uptake over the previous twenty years by an impressive communications apparatus that promoted a utopian vision of individual and corporate freedom unchained from government. This radical "neoliberal" alternative to Keynesianism was developed and promoted by networks of academics, business elites, think tanks and political organizations following the thinking of Austrian economists Ludwig von Mises, and more importantly, Friedrich Hayek, who published his popular masterpiece *The Road to Serfdom* in 1944.

The Rise of Neoliberal Free-Market Mania

Before Adam Smith came along, support for limiting government intervention in business affairs had already emerged as a core element of liberal thought in Europe, spreading from *laissez faire* thinking in France. In many ways, Adam Smith codified and extended those ideas and added his signature philosophy about norms and moral responsibilities in market societies in his classic work *The Wealth of Nations*. Tensions between monarchies and merchant communities sparked revolutionary ideas in England, the United States and France, and spinoffs of *laissez faire* thinking sparked critiques of colonialism during the mid to late 1800s. A more familiar reframing that begins to resemble contemporary neoliberal economics gained prominence after World War I with the founding of the International Chamber of Commerce (ICC). That body waged a large-scale campaign, particularly in the victorious allied nations of the US, France, and Britain, to grant business greater freedom and protection to operate internationally through trade agreements, property protections, and dispute settlement mechanisms. The ICC campaigned during the 1920s around the themes of "merchants of peace" and "world peace through free trade."[3] However, the interwar years in Europe proved too turbulent politically to implement this vision. Even in the more stable democracies such as the US and Britain, the idea of limited, business friendly governance was soon displaced by the spread of Keynesian economics during the Great Depression and the necessity of government management of wartime economies after that.

The core ideas of limited government, free markets, and individualism resurfaced again in 1938, just before World War II, at *The Walter Lippmann Colloquium* in Paris. This gathering of 26 select "economists, philosophers, sociologists, civil servants, business executives, and jurists" was convened by French philosopher Louis Rougier to discuss Walter Lippmann's *The Good Society*.[4] The participants shared a concern that the foundations of liberalism were threatened an all sides by fascism, communism, and, in the democracies, by the Keynesian approach to state-managed economies. Lippmann's book was a timely defense of liberal values of individual freedom, private property, and the limited role of government. Although the war disrupted the momentum of this group, it was clear that an impressive brain trust was available to develop these ideas.

After the war, a new gathering was convened by Friedrich Hayek, who had attended the earlier Lippmann seminar. The group that assembled in 1947 at the Swiss town of Mont Pelerin included Hayek and Ludwig von Mises, along with future Nobel economics laureates Milton Friedman and George Stigler, along with philosopher Karl Popper and some thirty other luminaries. After exploring various names, the group settled on the relatively inconspicuous Mont Pelerin Society (MPS), which has continued to meet regularly since then in various locations around the world.

Although the Lippmann Colloquium embraced the neoliberal terminology, the postwar group followed Hayek's concern that labels often obscure rather than clarify ideas, while offering convenient targets for enemies, so the network has largely refrained from using the neoliberal label for its brand of thought. The present-day statement on the official MPS website simply identifies a set of core principles such as defending political and economic liberalism, and fighting the dangers of "the expansion of government, not least in state welfare, in the power of trade unions and business monopoly, and in the continuing threat and reality of inflation."[5]

In his provocative essay "The Political Movement that Dared Not Speak Its Own Name," Philip Mirowski explored the resistance to self-labeling by this movement and observed how the use of innocuous terms such as libertarianism have conveniently obscured its importance – and even its existence. It has not helped that critics on the left have used the term neoliberal as something of an epithet, and in ways that sound almost conspiratorial.[6] This has made it easy to accuse leftist critics of misplaced name-calling, even as the core neoliberal precepts and their national variations have become more pervasive. This aversion to labeling, combined with the broad uptake of its ideas supports the perverse utopian claim that we have simply entered a natural state of being.

With these caveats, I use the term neoliberal for its analytical value in at least two senses. First, many of the key thinkers from the Lippmann Colloquium, to the MPS, and throughout many scholarly and journalistic circles since, have claimed a revival of eighteenth-century liberal thought, particularly in Adam Smith's ideas about markets, and John Locke's thinking about the primary role of government to protect private property and limit unruly passions of the people. A second, and more important sense in which neoliberal is a useful analytical concept is to point out how current reinventions often distort original liberal thinking. For example, Smith was a moral philosopher who wrote about the responsibility of business interests to society, and the role of governments to introduce fairness in markets. Much of this moral basis of classical liberal thought has been modified and even abandoned in neoliberal action.

Although Hayek would not have approved of the degree of business corruption of politics and markets in recent years, he noted in various publications that authoritarian regimes could be compatible with his economic principles and were in many cases preferable to democracies that imposed restrictions on property and markets. During his visit to Chile under the Pinochet dictatorship he overlooked the humanitarian transgressions of the regime and offered the view that the dictatorship was a transition between what he regarded as the democratic totalitarianism of the popularly elected Allende regime that Pinochet overthrew, and a more limited liberal democracy of the future. In an interview in the Chilean paper *El Mercurio* in 1981, Hayek remarked: "Personally, I prefer a liberal dictator to a democratic government lacking in liberalism."[7] The point here is not to become embroiled in the often bitter debates waged by latter-day adherents of rational choice and public choice theories in the social sciences who protect their neoliberal views from such unpleasant associations. Rather, the point is that terms like liberalism or libertarianism are inadequate to explain the uneasy relationship between neoliberal capitalism and democracy.

Thanks to the idea production and political networking strategies described in the next sections, the belief that truth and justice lie in free markets gradually became a utopian bible for the radical transformation of society and politics by severely restricting government management of the economy and provision of social welfare. The early adopters of this thinking, beyond the handful of economists who were Hayek disciples, were many business elites who mixed fact and fantasy by championing both the heroic libertarian novels of Ayn Rand, and the utopian economic appeal of Hayek. There has been far less attention paid to the amount of government intervention required to implement national versions of those programs, or the resulting business corruption of governments that ensued. Nonetheless, simplified and ultimately deceptive versions of these ideas were easy to sell in the early stages, given the critical economic conditions of the time. Both Thatcher and Reagan, among other center-right politicians, spread hopeful fantasies of individuals and enterprises being freed from onerous taxes and other government restraints, and thus able to compete and consume without restriction or moral reservation. Growth, of course would be unchained once more. Reagan called it "morning in America." Thatcher simply announced: "there is no alternative."

This wave of change soon swept the politics of most nations, until even center-left parties yielded to the vicious spiral of market pressures and compelling individual freedom narratives to reduce worker protections and downsize the public sector. The formation of the World Trade Organization in 1995 institutionalized the principles of market fundamentalism, intellectual property protections, business-dispute settlement, and disregard for workers and environment, throughout much of the world. As George Monbiot put it, this neoliberal revolution involved: "... massive tax cuts for the rich, the crushing of trade unions, deregulation, privatization, outsourcing, and competition in public services. Through the IMF, the World Bank, the Maastricht Treaty, and the World Trade Organization, neoliberal policies were imposed – often without democratic consent – on much of the world. Most remarkable was the political uptake of versions of those ideas among parties that once belonged to the left: the UK Labour and the US Democrats, for example."[8] Stedman Jones, who chronicled this spread of disruptive ideas remarked that "it is hard to think of another utopia to have been as fully realized."[9]

As Philip Mirowski, Dieter Plehwe, and others have noted, the influence of this initially rather small but powerful group, with its many national and international think tank, academic, business, and political networks, has been profound. The social, political, economic, cultural, psychological, and environmental embedding of ideas from this movement continue to be found hiding in plain sight. This is likely the most influential movement that most people have never heard of. Yet various forms of neoliberalism have become institutionalized around the world.

How did such an unlikely and predatory set of ideas gain so much staying power? And what lessons can be learned from this ongoing chapter of history about how a more society-and-planet-friendly political economy can be communicated more effectively? These are timely questions, as the contemporary rise of trade wars, the revival of nationalism, the backlash against globalism from the radical right, and the general weakness of many national economies, all present opportunities for change, for better or worse. The contrast between governments of developed nations that performed relatively well during the Covid-19 pandemic (South Korea, Taiwan, New Zealand, Australia, Germany, and most of the Nordic Countries) and those that failed (Spain, Italy, UK, and US) offer lessons about the hollowing of state capacity in more and less advanced neoliberal regimes.

The economic aftermath of Covid-19 provided openings to move toward more resilient societies and economies, but the degree to which significant change can occur depends importantly on whether progressive movements learn to communicate and organize around shared ideas. This is a long-term project, but without such a shift the shock doctrine will continue as the most common response to crisis opportunities, and economic growth is likely to remain the secular religion of our time – with economists playing the roles of priests and prophets, and the media providing the megaphone. Even neo-Keynesian economists who see the flaws in the current system talk gloomily of "secular stagnation," meaning a long-term failure to grow despite continuing low interest rates, debt, and other stimuli used to manage a "normal" economy.

The idea-flow model introduced earlier in the book offers a useful framework for understanding how this movement with no name became successful and why neoliberalism has proved so difficult to dislodge, despite its failures in theory and practice, and the growing unpopularity of many of its core ideas. An important point of this analysis is to identify aspects of the communication and organization of the neoliberal movement that progressive movements can adapt to the development of more equitable and ecologically resilient economies.

The Production of Neoliberal Ideas

During the reign of Keynesianism, Friedrich Hayek worked at the London School of Economics. After the war, the popularity of *The Road to Serfdom* brought him to wider public attention. He was visited at LSE by Anthony Fisher, a rich chicken magnate who opposed the spread of Keynesianism and democratic socialism. He was taken with Hayek's ideas about markets, truth, and human freedom. Fisher said he wanted to go into politics to promote that doctrine. Hayek discouraged him by talking about the greater impact he could have by using his wealth and connections to produce ideas in coordinated ways through think tanks that would connect "experts" with journalists and politicians. Hayek thought of intellectuals and the think tanks that would spread their ideas to politicians, press, and publics as "secondhand dealers in ideas." This was not a disparaging term, but a fundamental insight into how to spread a set of controversial and previously marginalized ideas that, given political uptake into party agendas and government policies, would profoundly limit the capacities of publics and governments to control economies for the larger good. Fisher's account of his early meeting included this advice from Hayek: "Keep out of politics and make your case to intellectuals – that is to teachers and the media – because they in turn influence the people ... He who makes public sentiment actually makes legislation possible."[10]

In 1955, Fisher founded what was to be the first of many neoliberal think tanks, the Institute of Economic Affairs. The IEA became highly influential in the UK by providing many ideas that helped the rise of Margaret Thatcher, and has continued to shape the British political economy through the production of propaganda urging separation from the European Union during the Brexit campaign. In order to help guide the transition after leaving the EU, the IEA set up a "Brexit Unit" to advise on economic policies.[11] Many of the post-Brexit IEA reports helped set the new political tone of the UK following the landslide election victory of the Tories in 2019. One widely circulated IEA study claimed that the BBC was biased in its Brexit coverage – a charge that provided ammunition for Prime Minister Boris Johnson's efforts to cut BBC budgets and license fees, and to force the broadcaster to move many of its operations away from London.

Similar think tanks soon developed in the United States, starting with the neoliberal shift in the already venerable American Enterprise Institute after Hayek disciple Milton Friedman joined its board in 1956. The production of influential ideas in the US continued with the Cato Institute funded by The Charles Koch Foundation. Koch, whose father Fred was a co-founder with Robert Welch of the radical John Birch Society, was another insider in the Mont Pelerin Society. The Cato Institute soon established ties with rising political star Ronald Reagan, as did the Manhattan Institute, which was founded in 1978 by William Casey and Anthony Fisher. Casey managed Reagan's presidential campaign in 1980 and become his CIA Director.

Following the early successes of the neoliberal idea factories in the US and the UK, Fisher understood that coordinated production of ideas was the secret to the rise of their movement. In 1981, he founded a global think-tank network, The Atlas Network, which at the time of this writing had grown to 475 organizations in over ninety nations.[12] The coordinated spread of neoliberalism has resulted in many different national and regional variants. As David Harvey observed, one of the advantages of neoliberalism over many other ideologies is that it is spare in its basic precepts and free of complex moral doctrine beyond the simple faith that truth and justice are found in free markets and private enterprise. Those thin ideological premises have enabled those simple precepts to become grafted onto many societies and political cultures, from the Pinochet dictatorship in Chile, to the capitalist authoritarianism of China, to many advanced democratic states.[13] Among the things that those varietals have in common, however, are diminished collective capacity to regulate markets and business, the socialization of risk, growing inequality, and the acceleration of environmental decline. In exchange, citizens were told that they gained great personal freedom, which translated mainly into greater lifestyle and consumer choice for the winners of the market game.

Few of these national-level idea production networks have been more effective than the political operations of the Koch brothers (Charles and the late David) in the US. Their idea production model that linked think tanks, political organizations, lobbying, and politicians was developed in helpful detail by Richard Fink, a follower of Hayek, who became a top advisor to Charles Koch and later became executive vice president of Koch Industries and president of the Koch Foundation. His widely circulated memo, "The Structure of Social Change," applied Hayek's thinking about manufacturing products to the manufacture of ideas. He outlined a model for mass producing ideas like commodities:

> Universities, think tanks, and citizen activist groups all present competing claims for being the best place to invest resources. As grant-makers, we hear the pros and cons of the different kinds of institutions seeking funding … Many of the arguments advanced for and against investing at the various levels are valid. Each type of institute at each stage has its strengths and weaknesses. But more importantly, we see that institutions at all stages are crucial to success. While they may compete with one another for funding and often belittle each

> other's roles, we view them as complementary institutions, each critical for social transformation ...
>
> The higher stages represent investments and businesses involved in the enhanced production of some basic inputs we will call "raw materials." The middle stages of production are involved in converting these raw materials into various types of products that add more value than these raw materials have if sold directly to consumers. In this model, the later stages of production are involved in the packaging, transformation, and distribution of the output of the middle stages to the ultimate consumers. Hayek's theory of the structure of production can also help us understand how ideas are transformed into action in our society. [14]

The production model begs the question of how the industrial ideas are packaged for delivery and sale to different target groups. Here, the methods may be of less value to those inhabiting evidence-based ideas, as they often involved concerted deception and "alternative truths" to hide the less palatable realities of growing inequality, limited democracy, and environmental damage. But those who can coordinate the production of ideas about more sustainable and people-friendly economies have an advantage that the neoliberals did not: ideas about better alignment of economy and environment are far more likely to receive popular support if packaged transparently.

Packaging Neoliberalism

Hayek watched the rise of labor politics and social democracy in Europe after World War I and concluded that the political climate was hostile to his ideas about privatization and market policy solutions. At the same time, he believed that truth was only found in markets, which possessed a collective intelligence that no individual or political faction could match. In order to attain this higher utopian truth, he concluded that the idea factories would package only part of the story for public consumption, while the darker aspects of limiting democracy and shrinking the welfare state would be delivered only to the core believers who saw such outcomes in more positive terms. This evolved into a doctrine of "double truth," as described by Philip Mirowski and Dieter Plehwe: "Hayek hit upon the brilliant notion of developing the "double truth" doctrine of neoliberalism – namely, an elite would be tutored to understand the deliciously transgressive Schmittian necessity of repressing democracy, while the masses would be regaled with ripping tales of "rolling back the nanny state" and being set "free to choose."[15] Carl Schmitt was a prominent German political theorist and legal scholar who promoted the idea of limiting the democratic power of the people in favor of strong states. He later joined the Nazi Party and provided legal and philosophical support for the transition from democracy to dictatorship.

As noted above, a core strategy of neoliberal communication has been to shift the idea of freedom from the political to the economic realm. This celebration of individual consumer and market freedom became the packaging for the otherwise unsellable ideas of market societies that catered to business, while producing growing inequality, individual precarity, and loss of popular sovereignty.

The legitimation of these troublesome ideas was aided greatly by efforts of intellectual zealots and wealthy funders to rebrand academic fields such as economics, political science, and public policy to valorize markets and individual choice, and problematize collective action and public welfare policies. In her book *Democracy in Chains*, Nancy MacLean documents how that new academic thinking was developed and spread with research programs funded in the US by Charles Koch through various Koch family foundations. That funding involved supporting the work of public choice theorist James Buchanan and the development of the Mercatus Center at George Mason University.[16] Although Hayek's ideas gained greater attention in their new academic packaging, Buchanan would come to resent being used to promote a political movement that drifted ever farther from the core principle that business should not corrupt government to distort markets. Despite the tension within the political wing of the movement, Buchanan's thinking provided a good deal of the mythology that business elites used to adorn their public image. Among the many gems still in circulation is the story about society being composed of a few entrepreneurial "makers," who required liberation from the majority of "takers" who depend on tax transfers and other forms of government support to prosper. Versions of that idea run through the novels of Ayn Rand and the myth has become inscribed in the daily language of business elites and conservative politicians and pundits. Following the successes of Buchanan and his colleagues at George Mason, Koch Foundation donations have since spread dramatically to other academic institutions. A Greenpeace study of tax records found that between 2005 and 2017, Koch Foundation funding to a long list of US universities totaled over $250 million.[17]

The packaging of neoliberal ideas gained even wider global appeal with the influence of a number of Nobel Prizes awarded to Friedrich Hayek, Milton Friedman, Gary Becker, Ronald Coase, and James Buchanan, among other Mont Pelerin Society members. A study by Offer and Söderberg suggests that the creation of the Nobel Prize in Economics in 1968, and its award to so many prominent neoliberals since, was an important factor in the rise of market liberalism as the leading idea to replace Keynesianism.[18] The Nobel award proved to be the most attractive package imaginable for an otherwise dubious set of ideas. The only notable democratic socialist economist to win the prize was the Swede Gunnar Myrdal, and only a few latter-day Keynesians such as Paul Krugman and Joseph Stiglitz have won.

The creation of the economics prize turns out to be among the most successful idea branding operations of all time, beginning with the seldom discussed fact that the economics award was not even part of the original Nobel bequest, which included prizes for physics, literature, chemistry, medicine and peace. The economics prize was created by the Swedish Central Bank as part of a campaign to gain greater independence from state and popular democratic control under a longstanding social democratic regime. Most of the awards went to scholars promoting economic theories based on the relative political independence of financial institutions and government market deregulation.[19] The official title of the award is "The Sveriges Riksbank Prize in Economic Sciences in Memory of Alfred Nobel." The bank made a large donation to the Nobel Committee to establish the prize, which soon became known as the Nobel Prize in Economics.[20] One of Alfred Nobel's descendants, Peter Nobel later said: "The Economics prize has nestled itself in and is awarded as if it were a Nobel Prize. But it's a PR coup by economists to improve their reputation."[21]

Packaging selected elements of neoliberalism differently for different audiences helps explain its broad appeal. Wrapping ideas about markets, lower taxes, and smaller government in images of consumer freedom worked well initially for many voters. The myth of makers and takers appealed to the vanity of business elites. Nobel Prizes added luster for a brand of economics that had long remained in the shadow of Keynesianism. Taken together, those different idea packages joined many citizens, business elites, and politicians in growing networks bent on separating economies from popular control.

Networking Neoliberalism

There are today many networks spreading variations on neoliberal thinking and related political initiatives, including the International Chamber of Commerce (ICC), which began the earlier mentioned efforts in the 1920s for market liberalization in democracies. Today the ICC represents 45 million businesses in one hundred nations.[22] This international federation is networked both internationally, with ties to the World Trade Organization and World Economic Forum, and nationally through in-country branches, that coordinate lobbying activities with business associations.

The intersection of many different national and international networks brings business and political elites together regularly in various conferences and gatherings such as the World Economic Forum, the Bilderberg Group, and the Mont Pelerin Society, along with numerous business associations and political organizations. This does not mean that all of these networks or their thousands of organizational and individual members agree on every principle or goal. As noted above, one of the strengths of the neoliberal movement that explains its embedding in so many different settings, is that the various branches have never agreed on a single vision or agenda. However, considerable agreement persists on core precepts such as independent central banking authorities, market deregulation, privatization of public functions, market solutions for public problems, and promoting elite rule in economic affairs.

The flexibility of these political networks is displayed in the Atlas Network, which remains one of the most important constellations in the neoliberal universe. The hundreds of Atlas Network think tanks feed ideas to many other networks and spread learning about managing various crises and political challenges. Today, the Atlas Network links to an expanding array of national and international think tanks, centers, and foundations that provide ideas, talking points, and drafts of legislation to politicians, while creating the appearance of public support with experts provided to the media, and astroturf (fake) organizations echoing their ideas from imaginary publics. A British environmental think-tank researcher observed how the proliferation of new institutes, centers, and foundations generates a 'constant river of commentary' from experts, ranging over topics such as Brexit and post-Brexit, climate change, and tax policy, creating the illusion that ideas that appeal to a tiny elite minority are actually more popular.[23] This public image provides cover for more radical rightwing politicians to gain power and prominence, resulting in politics increasingly out of synch with the public interest and the crises of our time.

The American branch of these global networks has been developed by various wealthy interests over many years. The names include DuPont, Mellon, Scaife, Mercer, DeVos, and Koch, among others. By far the most important contemporary promoter of the neoliberal state in the US has been the billionaire industrialist Charles Koch, introduced earlier in connection with his prominent role in the Mont Pelerin Society. The Koch network alone includes prominent academic institutes, think tanks, dozens of national and state level political organizations, political campaign finance operations, support for political movements such as the Tea Party, and the funding of various media operations.

As with the UK and other national networks, the American web of neoliberalism is aimed ultimately at government policy makeovers in areas ranging over environmental deregulation

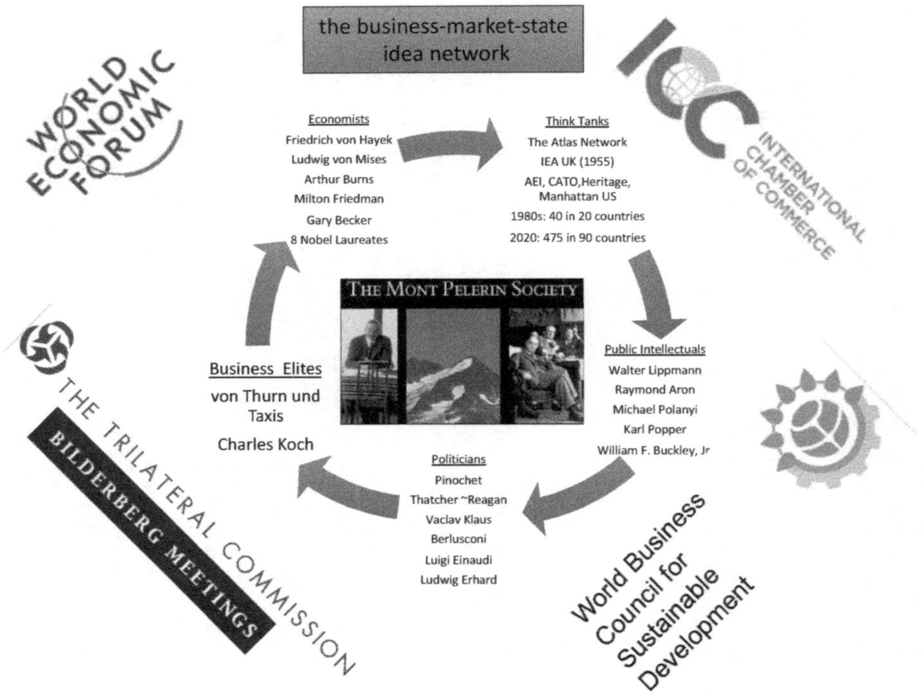

Figure 3.1 The Global Neoliberal Ideas Network

(Koch industries are major and unrepentant polluters), campaign finance, influencing political appointments, and restrictions on popular participation in elections. When Jane Mayer began reporting on these dense networks that have come to be known as "the Kochtopus," she was trolled and smeared by a team of Koch operatives, who tried to discount and deny the extent of Koch disinformation and political corruption operations detailed in her well-documented book *Dark Money*.[24]

The dense national and international networking of neoliberalism, with its environmentally unfriendly politics, is likely the most sophisticated influence and power operation on the planet today. Figure 3.1 sketches just the surface outlines of this global network.

Political Uptake

The inclusion of so many powerful business and political elites in these dense networks helps explain the persistence of neoliberal policies despite their growing dysfunction in environmental, economic, and democratic terms. Departing from this destructive path in the present day has become further complicated by a marriage of convenience between the persistent belief in the necessity of growth, and the core neoliberal achievements of deregulation of business sectors, politicians who restrict economic choices offered to voters, and limited government.

Growth – with little regard for what sort – has been combined with the political and social embedding of neoliberalism to remove popular control over economies. The continuing popularity of the idea of economic growth, combined with diminished popular political input in economic affairs, help explain why neoliberalism became so successful, and why it continues to lurch from crisis to crisis in its current zombie forms. This elevation of economy above democracy began with the dismantling of labor movements and unions since the 1980s and continued through the neoliberal turn of center-left parties in the 1990s. This great power shift runs through the present day, with diminished cohesion of citizen membership organizations in civil society, the rise of a professionalized civil society of NGOs to manage growing problems in the wake of government downscaling, and the corresponding fragmentation of the left across many issue and identity differences.

It is important to recognize that political uptake on the scale that neoliberalism has achieved did not just reshape politics and economics, but society itself. Stephen Metcalf captures this embedding in all areas of social life:

> Peer through the lens of neoliberalism and you see more clearly how the political thinkers most admired by Thatcher and Reagan helped shape the ideal of society as a kind of universal market (and not, for example, a polis, a civil sphere or a kind of family) and of human beings as profit-and-loss calculators (and not bearers of grace, or of inalienable rights and duties). Of course, the goal was to weaken the welfare state and any commitment to full employment, and – always – to cut taxes and deregulate. But "neoliberalism" indicates something more than a standard rightwing wish list. It was a way of reordering social reality, and of rethinking our status as individuals. Still peering through the lens, you see how, no less than the welfare state, the free market is a human invention. You see how pervasively we are now urged to think of ourselves as proprietors of our own talents and initiative, how glibly we are told to compete and adapt. You see the extent to which a language formerly confined to chalkboard simplifications describing commodity markets (competition, perfect information, rational behaviour) has been applied to all of society, until it has invaded the grit of our personal lives, and how the attitude of the salesman has become enmeshed in all modes of self-expression. In short, "neoliberalism" is not simply a name for pro-market policies, or for the compromises with finance capitalism made by failing social democratic parties. It is a name for a premise that, quietly, has come to regulate all we practise and believe: that competition is the only legitimate organizing principle for human activity.[25]

Those seeking change in societies like this might do well to learn some of the lessons of the rise of neoliberalism, particularly the production, packaging, and networking of attractive visions of change from which different local and national variants can emerge. Continuing discussions of carbon taxes or market solutions coming from Davos will neither sway public opinion, nor solve our problems. This may be our last opportunity for more meaningful change that can help ease the coming environmental disasters.

The Problem of Post-Democracy

In thinking about the rise of neoliberalism, one of its most influential proponents, Milton Friedman, made the simple observation that, "only a crisis – actual or perceived – produces real change. When that crisis occurs, the actions that are taken depend on the ideas that are lying around. That, I believe, is our basic function: to develop alternatives to existing policies, to keep them alive and available until the politically impossible becomes the politically inevitable."[26] Indeed, that is the story told so far in this chapter. Translating this story into more positive terms goes something like this:

> Until advocates for more progressive economic and environmental politics can produce well-crafted ideas in attractive packages that lend themselves to dense networking in social and political circles – until then, the uptake of good ideas to address environmental disaster will wait until long after the disaster defies imagination.

Advocates for change may take heart in the many contradictions and opportunities emerging in the present moment. As Joseph Stiglitz observed in the early days of the global financial crisis (now termed the Great Recession): "Neo-liberal market fundamentalism was always a political doctrine serving certain interests. It was never supported by economic theory. Nor, it should now be clear, is it supported by historical experience."[27] The contradiction of neoliberalism that seems to draw the greatest attention from both the left and the populist right is the legacy of business market fixing with the help of political corruption and related government deregulation. Those developments were highly undesirable in Hayek and company's utopian vision. The contradiction between neoliberal theory and political practice led to a falling out between Charles Koch and Murray Rothbard, who led other intellectual purists at the outset of the Koch's Cato Institute. According to one account, the originator of the term "Kochtopus" was a Rothbard follower, who similarly reviled the corruption of Hayek's free-market vision by what these critics called a "corporatist" market created by an unholy business–government alliance.[28]

The utopian Hayek vision of free markets and restricted government contained few answers for the problem of business corruption of government and markets. It is telling that following the Great Recession, many free-market idealists expressed shock that investment bankers whose fraud created the global financial crisis would violate the interests of their companies and shareholders to turn quick but disastrous profits. For example, Alan Greenspan chaired the US Federal Reserve Bank in the years leading up to the crisis. Greenspan was an insider in Ayn Rand's intellectual circle, and a self-proclaimed convert to the free-market gospels. When he was questioned by Congress about how the collapse could have happened, he confessed shock at finding a flaw in the ideology that had guided his thinking for the past forty years, saying: "... those of us who have looked to the self-interest of lending institutions to protect shareholders equity, myself especially, are in a state of shocked disbelief."[29] He went on to tell the committee that everyone must have an ideology in order to operate in the world, and that, despite the market collapse and its challenge to his belief system, he could not imagine a better alternative.

And yet, the institutionalization of corruption may now be the norm in many economies, as noted by James Galbraith who said that the crisis:

> ... exposed structural failings in the financial system, including hypertrophy, megalomania, predatory competition, bad judgment, and massive levels of fraud. Mainstream economists denied that such problems were possible. Widespread fraud, they reasoned, could be ruled out on the basis of the reputational risk to the fraudster. (These same economists also relied on models in which the financial sector essentially did not exist.) In the real world, the exact opposite is true: the more fraudulent you are, the more successful you become, at

least until you are exposed. Every country has oligarchs of this type. Generally speaking, once a system built on fraud, self-dealing, and poor judgment has been exposed, it cannot be repaired except through aggressive, comprehensive reforms, and the administration of justice. In the case of the 2008 crisis, that did not happen. The financial system was patched up, and existing institutions remained in place. Very little was done to reform them, and many of the same people were left in charge. Almost no one was prosecuted. The upshot is that we now have a financial sector that is structurally incapable of providing strategic direction to the real economy. Global finance is the sick man of capitalism. As with the Ottoman Empire before 1914 and the Soviet Union in the 1980s, its weaknesses are felt far and wide, and those who peer into the future do not believe that the future is very bright.[30]

Another contradiction that may help strengthen collective resolve for change is the dark antidemocratic politics of neoliberalism. David Harvey observed: "While individuals are supposedly free to choose, they are not supposed to choose to construct strong collective institutions (such as trade unions) as opposed to weak voluntary associations (like charitable associations). They most certainly should not choose to associate to create political parties with the aim of forcing the state to intervene in or eliminate the market."[31] Thanks to the institutionalization of such contradictions, there are ample signs of things flying apart at the seams. As noted above, the many years of market deregulation have not produced more perfect competition, as much as political capture and oligopolistic market manipulation in many business sectors.

Tension in neoliberal networks has also built up around the rise of rightwing nationalism and the populist backlash against globalism. In some cases, this has resulted in nationalist versions of neoliberalism, as witnessed in the Brexit campaign, with its successful disinformation strategies developed partly with the help of the Institute of Economic Affairs. The IEA and other think tanks provided politicians such as Boris Johnson and the tabloid press with scripts outlining why the European Union overly restricted British economic freedom and control over citizenship. As mentioned earlier, after the official departure from the EU, the IEA later created a Brexit Unit to make sure that the new national course would involve even less regulation and government bureaucracy, and, one suspects, even more political favors out the back door of 10 Downing Street.

It is ironic that the critique of neoliberal globalization began with the left in the 1990s and has now moved to the right with the rise of nationalist movements against various "globalist" conspiracies. These movements on the right present different challenges to the corporate neoliberal vision than earlier attacks from the left. The rise of politicians such as Donald Trump in the US, or Boris Johnson and the Brexit adventure in the UK, were not envisioned by many business interests in the global political–business alliance.

The latter-day Davos crowd likely prefer the rosier times of the 1990s, when publics were more easily sold on the benefits of global trade and international economic arrangements. These and other tensions can now be seen inside the World Economic Forum, where discussions are increasingly multi-focal, and at odds with thinking on the radical right about issues such as climate change. For example, the 2020 WEF meeting included a speech from Greta Thunberg, who urged leadership in wealthy nations to act more decisively and support poorer nations that are heavily impacted. Meanwhile, at the same meeting, Donald Trump attacked climate activists as "prophets of doom." Also attending that meeting was Christiana Figueres, who led the 2015 Paris climate agreement and promoted her Mission 2020 agenda for better aligning business, political, and environmental interests among the world elites. She condemned Trump and other obstructionists and pointed to the global risk report issued by the WEF that listed the top five economic threats as environmental – ranging over climate change, ecosystem deterioration, species loss, sea level rise, and life-threatening pollution. Even if Trump was in a minority at the meeting, and the populist right has not yet overturned global corporate alliances, the best we can expect from the Davos crowd will continue to involve market solutions and business friendly approaches to the environmental crises.

Managing the environmental crisis should not be left to currently configured business and political elites, but there is hope in the fact that some prominent leaders are beginning to awaken to the flaws of the current system. This may be a good time to remember that capitalism has been adapted to different political and social ends over its history. And not so long ago, business and wealthy interests were pressured in most democracies to take less indulgent deals than the ones they have cut for themselves recently.

What is missing in this moment is the lack of a compelling economic critique and alternative model around which to organize political change. There are of course calls for a revival of democratic socialism, as expressed variously from politicians such as Bernie Sanders in the US, or in the writings of Naomi Klein. However, this is not the time for ideological revivals that will not be palatable even for many on the left today, not to mention being unacceptable to more general publics who might be drawn to less ideological and more commonsense ideas.

Rather than fight a losing battle to replace capitalism, it makes more sense to think about how to communicate, deploy, and assess more pragmatic economic models that focus on: more social investment and less speculation; changing taxes and other incentives to better distribute economic outputs; less worrying about growth for its own sake, and, of course, production and consumption systems that sever ties with fossil fuels and other toxics. Even more important than the specifics of any model for a new political economy, which will vary from place to place, is the question of how civil-society organizations and political party factions can organize ways to produce, package, network, and promote the uptake of better ideas. Until a more effective politics emerges, the scenarios for many democracies point toward illiberal outcomes where ethnic nationalism meets crony capitalism. The hope is for idea production networks to develop a more compelling economic critique that is free enough of ideological baggage to appeal to large publics and political leaders.

4

Democracy with a Future: Mobilizing Ideas and Opportunities for Change

Finding effective ways to address the current crisis is a tall order with a great species extinction in progress, and billions of people being pushed farther to the limits by deteriorating environmental conditions. To make matters worse, the most palpable political trend under way in the democracies is the rise of rightwing nationalism. So far in this century the right has done much better than the left in elections in many democracies, enabling the spread of disinformation and obstructing climate action. Donald Trump in the US and Jair Bolsonaro in Brazil quickly rolled back years of hard-won progress on environmental protections as discussed below. How can we assess the democratic imbalance between the right and the left and understand the opportunities for change?

Developments on the right are transforming the meaning and practice of twentieth-century conservatism with reactionary perspectives that amplify social divisions and threaten hard-fought political struggles over race, religion, sexuality, immigration, and citizenship itself. This global radical right movement has also produced and spread disinformation through think tanks, parties, and other political organizations, with the aim of blocking action on climate change. The combination of global propaganda networks, the election of reactionary politicians, and the easy spread of lies on social-media platforms, all appeal to many citizens who embrace nostalgic visions of passing lifestyles and simpler societies. In the United States, even the Covid-19 pandemic of 2020 became politicized and culturally coded, with Trump and the rightwing media downplaying the seriousness of the health threat and playing up the importance of getting the economy going again. Some even called for older people to sacrifice themselves for the good of the economy and the nation. Trump's daily briefings on the situation turned into streams of disinformation that sent concerned health professionals and public officials into damage control mode. It eventually dawned on many observers that those media events had replaced Trump's campaign rallies during an election disrupted by the spread of the virus.

Waves of manufactured confusion have spilled into the mainstream press in most democracies, due in part to elected politicians who deliver messages that resonate with their followers. Tools such as fact checking do little to blunt the point of disinformation. And until more effective regulatory solutions are found, social-media companies such as Facebook will continue to resist serious policing of fake accounts and inflammatory falsehoods that have become front lines in battles for public attention.

Most readers of this book probably believe that democracy, involving some meaningful popular influence over public agendas and important decisions, is inherently a good thing. But too often these days, politicians offer citizens a mix of emotional and pragmatic issues such as immigration, religion, taxes, jobs, schools, health, race, leaving the European Union, or restoring national sovereignty by rescuing the people from corrupt globalist elites. When communication environments are infused with fear, disinformation, division, and encouragement to live in the moment, democracies and their contemporary post-democracy variants are unlikely to produce great intelligence or foresight.

A major question facing democracies today is how to grapple with great disruptions and do something meaningful about the rapidly deteriorating quality of life on the planet. Part of the answer, developed in this chapter, is for civil-society movements and political parties to develop more people-and-planet-friendly economics, and learn to communicate those ideas to voters. One might think this would be easier, given the number of center-left traditional parties (e.g. European Social Democrats and Christian Democrats, UK and Australian Labour, US Democrats) that are trying to reinvent themselves, yet continue having trouble attracting voters with effective messages. One obvious obstacle is that most of those parties, to varying degrees, have been captured by business pressures not to rock the economic boat. This means that citizens and movement groups need to become insurgent forces pressuring and supporting those parties. This of course requires that organizations currently scattered across thousands of issues and ideas must find ways of developing and sharing more workable economic ideas that can benefit all of their missions.

Those forces for change can shape and monitor what goes into hopeful sounding packages such as the European Union's "European Green Deal." In announcing the initiative, EU President Ursula von der Leyen promised a new growth strategy that "gives back more than it takes away" by showing how to "transform our way of living and working, of producing and consuming, so that we live healthier lives and make our businesses innovate."[1] While those words sound good, the idea-flow model suggests that the outcomes depend on organized political networks pressing for uptake of transformative policy specifics. Without such pressure from below, it is unlikely that the initiative will strike the best balance between people, planet, and business.

Beyond the realignment of civil-society organizations, it would also help for consumers and investors to use their considerable leverage to condition big business to behave more responsibly – or at least not block the economic changes needed for long-term survival. It is time for more visible public discussion of how to adjust the foreshortened time frame of business, along with the ceaseless pursuit of profits and growth at any cost. A core idea here is that it is long past time to continue converting natural resources into paper wealth that competes directly with long-term life values. This echoes the ideas of John Stuart Mill from Chapter 2, who would also urge us to add that it is time to reassess our social values and remember that money is a means to social progress, not an end.

All of this requires those who fund politics, from investing in candidates, to supporting think tanks and political organizations, to streamline and better coordinate their agendas. Funders must develop strategies to incentivize a convergence of ideas among political organizations and to promote them with better network organization and more concerted action. In this regard, funders interested in changing the game can learn many lessons from their counterparts on the right, as discussed in the last chapter, and in more detail below.

While all of this may seem like a tall political order, it cannot loom much larger than the challenge that faced the rightwing in many nations, particularly in the US, in the mid twentieth century. As discussed in the last chapter, the neoliberal agenda was developed during a period when Keynesian economics prevailed, labor was strong, and conservative parties were struggling to find popular messages. Yet, in a relatively short time, a new brand of neoliberal political economy began to spread around the world, thanks to the opportunities provided by the collapse of the Keynesian order, and the opportunistic positioning of alternatives because of how the neoliberal movement managed the flow of its ideas. This chapter charts a path forward for positioning better alternatives to this brand of predatory capitalism to take advantage of ongoing economic and environmental crises. The communication and organizational strategies suggested here borrow selectively from the strategies used by the neoliberal right in its rise to global dominance in a relatively short period of time. There are of course both political and historical differences that must be addressed, suggesting that a good beginning point is to review the current political landscape.

The Political Future at a Crossroads

One thing seems clear, at least to those who belong to the evidence-based community: the clock on a livable future is ticking, and conditions are growing far worse. Even if it is too late to prevent many disasters from happening, it is not too late to make them less terrible. Thus, it helps to avoid thinking and talking about the crisis in all or nothing terms that suggest either that we must act immediately, or that it is already too late to do anything. It is simply not possible to wave a political wand and produce sweeping remedial action now. And yet, the sound that comes most clearly from the growing protests around the world is a plaintiff cry to "Do something now!" But it is clear most parties and governments are burdened with the neoliberal legacy of hollowed out states, compounded by the effects of the Covid-19 pandemic. What is missing is a widely shared program of action with personally engaging narratives that people can imagine stepping into. Until more coordinated communication networks are developed to produce and spread ecological economics, the continual sounding of alarms, followed by inaction will only invite people to think it is already too late and that we are doomed.

Nonetheless, in order for real change to occur in democracies, several key political dysfunctions found to varying degrees in different nations must be addressed: inequality, representation deficits, business capture of government, and parties replacing public interest agendas and leadership with political branding and election marketing. As noted earlier, these are among the factors cited by Crouch as marking the category shift from democracy to post democracy.[2] In light of these problems it is no wonder that scholars are raising concerns about democratic capacities in many nations. In her provocative book *Can Democracy Be Saved?* Donatella della Porta discusses many of these problems, including the implications for electoral democracy when so many activists and movements on the left have adopted direct, deliberative models of democracy that do not interface well with parties and elections.[3] In earlier work, della Porta noted a shift in movement activism from more conventional, organizationally led and brokered coalitions to more flexible associations of individuals gathering in vast networks of networks of networks that disperse rather than focus ideas.[4]

My own research with Alexandra Segerberg and Curd Knüpfer has explored participation trends in EU nations during the first two decades of this century. We found higher levels of political participation on the radical left than the radical right in all modes of political action except one:

voting. We conclude that the growth of issue and identity politics on the left reinforces a political culture of direct, participatory, and deliberative politics that works better outside of electoral settings.[5] These trends have developed over many years, beginning in the 1980s and 1990s with protests against neoliberalism and globalization. Early global justice communities such as World Social Forum meetings struggled over whether the many factions should form a grand movement with an overarching political and economic agenda, or whether it was best to create safe communication spaces to nurture a culture of diversity and inclusion. Those critical struggles seem to have been largely settled in favor of the ethos of diversity and inclusiveness, with little consensus on how, or whether, to form grand coalitions to carry common messages into national politics. In this context, it is no small irony that neoliberal regimes have produced growing lists of problems and social fragmentation that have become mirrored in the fragmenting efforts of the left to somehow address them all, often as categorically discrete issues. Many on the left have of course recognized this problem, but thus far none of the initiatives to address it has gained much traction (e.g. Democracy in Europe Movement 2025, or Momentum in the UK).

Societies have changed in many ways since the twentieth-century times of grand social movements that pressurized parties for progressive reforms. However, it is possible to imagine updated versions of those collective action models better suited to more flexible connective action in contemporary networked societies. As suggested in Chapter 1, the model of organizationally enabled networks that share ideas and stabilize action agendas seems a good fit with contemporary political conditions. Added to this, the idea-flow model may offer a beginning point for diverse organizations to develop and share an economic critique with an alternative political vision better suited for environmental and economic security.

Developing an appealing economic vision that promises a more viable environmental future, and finding strategies for successful political uptake, may seem nearly impossible under the current political constraints. However, in many ways it is no less likely than the prospects of neoliberalism replacing Keynesianism after its reign from the 1930s until the late 1960s. Indeed, the neoliberal leader Milton Friedman proclaimed in 1965, "we are all Keynesians now" – a phrase often attributed to Richard Nixon, who said something similar during the financial crisis of 1971. What Friedman meant was that the idea of state-managed economies and regulated markets had become so pervasive that it provided the standard vocabulary and set of policy tools for politicians and policymakers around the world. What Friedman went on to point out was the irony that, although pervasive, Keynesian approaches no longer seemed to work. The pervasiveness of Keynesianism belied a reality in which economies and world finance no longer responded to its core ideas. The key factor in the uptake of neoliberal ideas was that they were well developed, packaged, and networked by the time the crisis provided the political opportunity.

A similar moment exists today. It might be said that we are all neoliberals now (although, many policymakers revert to Keynesian actions in times of crisis). Ideas related to market solutions and limited government have become pervasive, but they belie a reality of economic dysfunction that resists known remedies beyond debt driven policies that threaten to proliferate zombie economies around the world. Where the 1970s witnessed the Keynesian impossibility of "stagflation," the present time is in the grip of what some economists are referring to as "secular stagnation." Secular in this sense refers to the persistent failure of economies to grow or respond to known economic remedies, short of structurally unsound measures such as debt-driven growth.

Since neoliberalism was not widely thought to be a contending idea system before it rose to such prominence, perhaps there are some things that we can learn from its historic uptake. And perhaps those lessons can be applied – with important modifications, of course – to thinking about how an alternative and more promising economic system might emerge to take its place. One thing is sure: there are no guarantees that good ideas will come along or insert themselves into the fabric of society and institutions when the need arises. There is little evidence that neoliberalism rose on its intellectual or moral merits. It was pushed into circulation through brilliant political communication strategies and organized political networking. Even though it has long outlived its moment, the quest to find solutions in markets persists largely because of the undue political power accrued by wealthy interests, and the use of that power to capture parties and to corrupt democratic and state institutions.

Some Political Lessons from the Rise of Neoliberalism

Idea systems that compete for attention and uptake generally require a combination of opportunity and clever political communication and organization strategies to attain dominance. If a different economic vision is to displace neoliberalism (and avoid its replacement by rightwing ethnic nationalism and/or authoritarian kleptocracies), different kinds of political communication and organization must emerge. Perhaps there are some lessons to be learned from how neoliberalism rose to power. Let's begin by reviewing some of the takeaways from the last chapter.

There are at least five key points about how neoliberalism in particular, and new ideas in general, gain uptake. We can think of this communication process in terms of the four stages of the *idea-flow model* introduced earlier in the book, along with a fifth element that often plays an important role in change processes: recognizing and taking advantage of *political opportunities*. To recap the lessons from the rise of neoliberalism, the spread of ideas that challenge leading societal paradigms generally entails: (1) producing alternative ideas coordinated among think tanks, academic experts, and civil-society organizations, (2) packaging those ideas so that different messages and narratives engage various audiences such as journalists, business communities, activists, politicians, and publics, (3) networking the spread of those ideas so that they diffuse through society, government, and business, (4) securing political uptake through movements and organized interests pressuring parties and governments to embed the new ideas in elections, policies, and governing institutions, and (here comes the new element), (5) using political opportunities such as crises that disrupt traditional elite and party alignments to insert the new ideas into both public and elite conversations about future directions. A review of each point illustrates how a different politics can benefit from this simple model of communication and political organization.

Lesson 1: The Coordinated Production of Alternative Ideas

Among the ingenious inventions of neoliberalism was the loose networking of national, local, and issue-specific think tanks, which enabled common themes to become translated for different audiences in different socio-political situations. The production of variations on core themes aimed at different target groups of idea consumers helped otherwise abstract ideological concepts seem natural in the wide range of contexts in which they were received and understood. More broadly, simple ideas about markets and private property translated into many diverse settings, from Chile during the military dictatorship of the 1970s and 1980s, to the United States during roughly the same period, when Americans were being encouraged by conservative politicians to seek tax relief, retreat from public life, and enjoy enhanced consumer lifestyles. The idea of "freedom" – the great cover story of neoliberalism – clearly meant different things to different stakeholders in different places.

One can imagine applying these lessons to themes of resilience, (food, health, economic) security, community, fairness, inclusion, and nature, among other progressive products. However, organizations seeking more positive changes must recognize that during the same period that neoliberalism developed its movement model, most progressive civil-society organizations managed to scatter their resources and attention over a profusion of issues. One ironic connection between the neoliberal right and the left is that as neoliberal doctrines and policies became embedded in the institutions of state and society, growing numbers of social problems were created, government responsibilities for them were shed, and thousands of NGOs and other community groups emerged to try to address them all. Recall that the political agenda of the neoliberal movement included limiting the democratic capacity of publics to act collectively. The current dispersion of movement organization and communication is ironically consistent with that goal.

Most nations today have multiple think tanks producing neoliberal solutions for all manner of social, economic, and political problems. But there are few comparable progressive think tanks with the capacity to produce, coordinate, and distribute new economic and political ideas. In addition, the turn toward direct deliberative democracy and the fraying of relations with parties and electoral politics are all undermining the political capacities of the left today. Not only are voting rates lower on the left than the right, but radical right parties have entered legislatures and governments far more than their counterparts on the left.[6]

The coordination of funding for achieving political focus in idea production has a great deal to do with this. In thinking about the underlying differences in political alignment on the left and the right, consider a comparative study of two influential donor organizations in the US: the Koch seminars and the Democracy Alliance (DA). These donor networks channel funds to issue organizations and think tanks to advance political agendas. Theda Scocpol and her colleagues have studied these organizations since their inception in the early 2000s. Both organizations are aimed at using funding strategically to shape the political landscape around different visions. However, the Koch seminars invite wealthy donors to fund projects approved and coordinated by the Koch political network, while the Democracy Alliance brings donors together with hundreds of different organizations operating in different issue sectors on the left. Where the Koch seminars offer a unified strategy and top-down funding directives aimed at coordination across think tanks, political strategy organizations, election campaigns, and legislative action networks at different levels of government, the Democracy Alliance more resembles a "bazaar" where funders can choose among many different issue organizations or think tanks operating primarily at the national level. The resulting differences in political coordination are striking: "As the Koch seminars have fueled a tightly integrated political machine capable of drawing national and state

Republican office holders and candidates toward the ultra-free-market right, the Democracy Alliance has orchestrated more limited results by channeling resources to large numbers of mostly nationally focused and professionally managed liberal advocacy and constituency groups."[7]

The authors conclude that the Koch strategy has been much more effective at introducing change in both the composition of state and national legislatures and in subsequently writing laws and regulatory policies. While the organizations funded by the DA have waged successful issue campaigns and changed various policies, they do not share an overarching set of common principles, and their specific gains are often challenged and reversed by Koch initiatives. Although the DA mission statement embraces broad categories of democratic participation, an economy for all, and a healthy planet, the actual meetings more resemble a funding competition among progressive causes, a sharp contrast to the Koch seminar process: "While DA conferences are crowded with speakers from separate organizations and issue networks, the Koch gatherings expose conservative wealth-holders and their spouses to libertarian and free-market ideas and outline the latest version of a regularly updated coherent strategy for shifting US political culture, politics, and policies toward the far economic right."[8] While it is clear that many progressive organizations would resist top-down coordination, there is considerable room for creating much better horizontal networking.

The current imbalance in political influence between the loosely connected left and the much more organized neoliberal right is partly due to the funding gap, which is considerable and growing. However, the more notable gap is in coordination strategies aimed at developing common ideas and political strategies: "Koch Seminars are not only raising greater sums than the Democracy Alliance, they are channeling those heftier resources to a more compact set of organizations directly controlled by the Koch network itself."[9]

The neoliberal right in the US, led by the Koch network and its coordinating organizations such as Americans for Prosperity have formed what amounts to a shadow political party, working both within and outside of the Republican

Party. This means that even when Republican voters move in directions not consistent with the agenda of the Koch network, as in the election of Donald Trump, the shadow party still operates to shape the outcomes. Although Trump may have ridiculed other candidates during the 2016 primaries for their dependency on Koch funding, after the election, Koch network sources helped staff the administration from cabinet level appointments to agency heads and judicial nominations. And, of course, Vice President Mike Pence was long a Koch ally.

The promotion of free-market economics and limited government is not so much aided by the intellectual merits of the ideas or their benefits to society. The prominence of the market paradigm is due more to the relentless coordination of efforts from leaders of a global economic movement who are able to amass funding and coordinate intellectual and political efforts. Despite the growing contradictions between the core idea of market societies and their lived experience for majorities of citizens, the neoliberal project continued to promote itself with new ideas. For example, the leading lights of the Mont Pelerin Society during the 1980s saw the continuing role of governments in managing societies as a kind of stealthy Orwellian encroachment on "individual" freedom. At the 1984 meeting of MPS, a group was formed to develop an "economic freedom index" to better measure these encroachments of states into markets and government limitations on the personal control over wealth. The group was the brainchild of Michael Walker of the Canadian Fraser Institute (an important member of the Atlas Network), and included Milton and Rose Friedman, who had become successful at promoting popular accounts of free-market virtues. Also involved were Nobel economist Douglas North, and Charles Murray who would later popularize a renewed linkage between race and IQ.

The group produced an Index of Economic Freedom (IEF) that has become widely publicized and used to rate nations and recommend policies since the mid 1990s. The IEF is housed at the Heritage Foundation in the US, and co-sponsored by *The Wall Street Journal*, giving it considerable brand visibility. The core measures include (low) tax rates, (high) monetary stability, (low) state social service loads, and (high) private property protections. Democracy and political freedoms do not enter into the equation. As a result, early winners on the freedom scale included Honduras and Guatemala under military dictatorships. Later standouts in the twenty-first century included Hong Kong and Chile, with two of the highest levels of economic inequality in the world, and more recently racked by popular rebellions seeking more meaningful democratic freedoms.

In 2018, the United States came in eighteenth, below the United Arab Emirates and Georgia. When the 2018 ratings were rolled out at the Heritage Foundation, US Commerce Secretary Wilbur Ross attended the ceremony and declared his hope that Trump administration tax cuts and rollbacks in environmental regulations would improve the American ranking.[10] It did not take long for Mr. Ross to get his wish, as the wave of gifts to business helped the US move up to the twelfth spot in 2019.

In contrast to the IEF, there have been many efforts to define and measure prosperity in more human and environmentally friendly terms, but they have lacked the same unified vision and widespread promotion. Consider, for example, one of the more prominent alternative measures of wellbeing, the Genuine Progress Indicator (GPI) developed by a team led by Herman Daly, who was introduced in Chapter 2 as pioneer of the steady state economy. Long a critic of the Gross Domestic Product (GDP) indicator as insensitive to social and environmental costs and benefits, Daly branded the GDP as treating the earth as "a business on liquidation, and enabling the slide into 'uneconomic growth,' where there is little relationship between GDP and social welfare."[11] As noted in Chapter 2, even Simon Kuznets, the inventor of GDP, warned that his crude measure of growth was no indicator of social wellbeing, and that nations should decide the kind and the degree of growth that made sense to them. The Genuine Progress Indicator considered both the environmental and social values of economic activity with the aim of making economics work for both people and planet on a sustainable basis. Even though GDP rose dramatically in many nations toward the end of the twentieth century, the GPI flatlined and often declined. Many elements that are measured by the GPI look like solid elements of a new economic narrative: leisure and family time, health quality, time spent commuting, educational opportunity, natural resource use and depletion, climate-change effects, air and water pollution, and levels of debt and social investment, among others.

There has been some progress toward implementing such alternative measures of wellbeing, including initiatives in Canada, the US state of Vermont, and the United Nations' promotion of a "gross national happiness" index. The measure that has gained the most traction internationally is the Human Development Index, created by economists Mahbub ul Haq and Amartya Sen, and deployed globally by the United Nations Development Program. The measures include education, life expectancy, and income, with more recent adjustments for inequality levels that suppress or improve the spread of those other factors.[12]

These alternative visions of prosperity continue to fall far short of attaining comparable levels of public awareness and political uptake as GDP. Part of the problem is that there is little formal coordination of the production and packaging of core ideas to yield simple and sharable stories that travel.

Lesson 2: Packaging Ideas for Change

Another important lesson from the success of the neoliberal movement is the clear packaging of personalized narratives that people and politicians could share, without engaging more technocratic discourses about markets, regulation, and the role of government. As discussed in Chapter 3, those simple popular narratives eventually turned out to be inconsistent with underlying political and economic realities. It was difficult to hide the basic principles of this elite movement, which were never likely to benefit majorities of people or fit comfortably with democratic politics. Compelling narratives for economic and environmental justice will surely be more transparent and likely to produce more satisfying experienced realities, but they still need to appeal to positive emotional concerns about security and wellbeing that can be packaged in ways that help people engage and share.

Much of the public discourse produced by the think tanks and distributed through the political organizations of the neoliberal movement was a utopian vision of freeing individuals and enterprises from the chains of government regulation. These themes were popularized in Friedrich Hayek's *The Road to Serfdom*, and in many writings from variously aligned thinkers such as Ayn Rand, Karl Popper, and Walter Lippmann. Politicians such as Margaret Thatcher began to shock many on the left with her pronouncements like "There is no such thing as society." She was referring to people who blame their problems on society and seek government solutions that create dependencies that undermine individual responsibility for solving their own problems.[13] Dismantling societies built on government engineering of health care, education, public spaces, or civic organizations was a prime political objective of the movement, although the realities differed from nation to nation depending on cultural and political constraints. In cases such as the US, government itself came under attack, as in Ronald Reagan's iconic pronouncement: "The nine most terrifying words in the English language are: "I'm from the government and I'm here to help."[14] These ideas appealed to large publics who wanted to pay lower taxes, stop supporting those on welfare, and limit government regulation of business.

As fundamental conflicts between deregulated markets and promised individual freedoms are now apparent, the time is ripe for alternative packaging of ideas about economic prosperity that better suits personal wellbeing and democratic politics. A more viable economic program requires coordinated production of easily sharable narratives aimed at forging emotional connections between politicians and publics. Beyond specific elements such as health, education, or environmental quality, those talking points need to be included in frameworks of problems and solutions that people can easily grasp. Many promising "problem" frames already exist by simply talking about familiar personal experiences in market societies: risk, insecurity, instability, rapid economic transformation, human replacement by automation, and neglect of environmental conditions that directly affect life and personal safety. In these contexts, elements of a new prosperity become the building blocks for solutions that people can talk about and vote for.

All of these specifics can be packaged in memes already in circulation such as a "Green New Deal." That package can become both popular and transformative if filled with specific policies framed in terms of greater personal security, more stable and rewarded work, protections against automation of jobs, and living in less hostile natural environments. Filling easily shared packages such as GND with such specifics can become the basis for an emerging program that builds clear connections between economics, environment, and democratic reform. The advantage of these intersectional narratives is that they nest simple solutions for widely experienced problems within broader visions of a more positive future, while showing that politics, economics and the environment are best considered together.

The relationship between packaging and the ideas inside is crucial to successful communication. Consider two different ways of packaging similar ideas about balancing economic activities with environmental and human needs: "degrowth" vs. "donut economics." Proponents of the idea of degrowth advocate "a form of society and economy which aims at the wellbeing of all, and sustains the natural basis of life."[15] While it is hard to argue with that as a positive vision of change, packaging it as "degrowth" is hard to share among majorities of citizens. Degrowth likely sounds negative to people who have not thought much about economics, and who have become conditioned to think that engineering economic growth is a good thing. Moreover, many who embrace the term degrowth also promote a fundamental critique of capitalism, which may well be in order, but also limits the appeal for broader publics who are new to thinking about remedies for economic and environmental problems. Even the web portal to the international degrowth network contains a defense of the term itself, addressing the criticism that it seems to be a limited way to package an otherwise attractive vision.[16]

Consider, by contrast, the almost self-explanatory term "doughnut economics." As discussed in Chapter 1, this easy-open packaging was developed by English economist Kate Raworth. Her basic idea is that human activity should be nested within the environment so that resources and wastes are balanced and used to provide human wellbeing by organizing governments and other institutions based on those values.[17] In addition to being intuitive and easy to explain, Raworth's ideas also point out that the growth imperative has little or no economic or logical justification. Growth has become a popular myth, and like most myths, it thrives in the absence of alternatives for people to share and organize around. The difference with degrowth theories is that talking about change processes does not logically begin with challenging the output side of the equation but rethinking the inputs, figuring out how to monitor resource use, and letting growth take care of itself, which might look different in differently organized economies.

The point here is that there are plenty of sound ideas with which to organize a political economy of sustainability. But those ideas remain scattered, poorly integrated into political organizations and movements, and lacking attractive packaging. All of this adds up to a very different ecology of ideas and action than one finds on the neoliberal right, where far more attention is paid to coordinating the production of ideas, packaging them for different audiences and purposes, and embedding them into organizations and institutions in different issue areas. It is not difficult to imagine positive economic ideas packaged in terms that: (a) engage feelings of personal security and belonging, (b) in societies with more functional economies, that (c) restore the value of public goods, and (d) inspire responsibilities to each other and to nature. All of these features can be built into sharable packages such as a Green New Deal. The next step involves strengthening the network organization required for these ideas to travel. Changes in networking strategies are also involved in the production process, which shows how these elements of idea flow interact with each other.

Lesson 3: Networking the Spread of Ideas

The ideas of limited government and market societies based on individualized risk and responsibility did not spread spontaneously. Beyond the importance of idea development in think tanks and academic fields, the spread of neoliberal ideas depended on their flow across more distant political networks such as libertarian movements, business associations, and media outlets that carried the word. This does not mean that neoliberalism was ever a monolithic or deeply defined ideology. Indeed, one of its great attractions was a high level of abstraction and under specification. As various observers such as David Harvey and Dieter Plehwe have pointed out, neoliberalism spread in part because it was a fairly abstract utopian vision that enabled details to be filled in according to different cultural, political, and economic constraints.[18]

It may seem strange to think of this elite enterprise as a movement, but it was nothing less. As shown in Chapter 3, many dense networks were connected through national and international conferences, meetings, and the creation of political organizations. As in any movement, there were differences and splits, but there were also strong leaders and an available supply of money from influential backers to guide political strategies.

Despite the unpopularity of austerity and instability, the movement continues to develop and spread updates for its visions of limited government, property protections and market deregulation. As shown in Figure 3.1, those core precepts have traveled widely into society and politics through various business and political networks such as the World Economic Forum, the Bilderberg meetings to coordinate and spread European and North American economic influence, and the International Chamber of Commerce and its related national networks with more than six million members in some one hundred countries. These and other networks exchange ideas and influence. Those networks also address (with mixed success) various contradictions and developments that threaten the legitimacy of free-market economics such as growing inequality and state corruption.

As noted above, the development of a political economy movement anchored in social and environmental values will differ in important ways, in particular, by featuring more empathic core values to less hierarchical messaging and deception. However, the strengthening of environmental, economic, and political change should become a much higher priority for funders and movement organizers. As noted earlier, I have tracked networked idea flows along various change networks in the US and Europe to see how ideas travel and whether they cross issue category divides. The findings thus far are not encouraging. For example, the New Economy Coalition (NEC) has made efforts to reach out to environmental organizations. NEC is a progressive network in the US that emphasizes economic justice, local transformation, and cooperatives. An initiative to bridge these ideas into environmental activism networks met with little observable success as measured by mapping linkages among organizations in the different networks and monitoring the content of traffic on email lists. A similar mapping exercise in Europe followed degrowth movement networks over several years, also with little notable growth or centralized coordination beyond the linking of different organizations to various conferences.

As discussed earlier, when diverse civil-society networks do converge, it is often with the explicit recognition and celebration of differences, based on norms that do not privilege particular issues or causes over others. Even in impressive mass protests involving large gatherings of the progressive political tribes, core issues often do not travel easily across the various communication networks that fan out from the core of the protests to the periphery. Peripheral networks are crucial in the spread of ideas, because they typically contain large numbers of people who can spread content into broader social circles. Recall, for example, a case mentioned in Chapter 1 involving the Occupy Wall Street protests in 2011–2012. The broad consensus among participants was to honor the dozens, even hundreds, of issues and causes represented by the protesters. However, many of the core activists and movement leaders were more concerned about banking regulation and democratic reform. As with many of the grand gatherings on the left, maintaining the scale of the protests depended on honoring the ethos of diversity and inclusiveness, rather than trying to forge a more coherent political agenda. As a result, many messages from the core of the protests did not travel coherently into society.

Meanwhile on the right, the US witnessed the rise of a Tea Party movement around the same time, with critiques of banks, government, and globalism echoed by radical nationalist movements in other democracies. Aided by a combination of financial resources and focused political organization (e.g. the Koch network in the US) that movement formed a much more streamlined issue agenda, and soon entered the Republican Party as an insurgent faction that changed the direction of the party itself, changes that were amplified by the election of Donald Trump. As noted in Chapter 3, the funders of the Tea Party began to lose control of their populist monster following with Trump's election, mirroring developments over the same period in Europe, as a number of radical right parties were either reenergized or newly formed. While the radical right seems headed for authoritarian solutions, the left remains unable to focus messages, consolidate networks, or reconstitute its electoral power.

Many progressive civil-society organizations have tried to develop networking strategies to mobilize support to their causes. In recent years there have been interesting experiments in which prominent organizations such as Oxfam have stepped back from the tendency to brand and own campaigns for their particular issues, in order to join with other organizations in creating loosely networked campaigns to engage publics around broader causes. As mentioned briefly in Chapter 1, after the financial crisis in 2008–2009, dozens of organizations in the UK, and beyond, developed a networking campaign called "Put People First" that invited individuals to share their experiences of the crisis, and join in pressuring authorities to put people ahead of the banks. Simple and personalized ideas about how economies could work better for people traveled widely in many nations during this period, spread with help from different networks of NGOs.[19]

Another case also briefly mentioned in Chapter 1 involved a similarly broad European NGO coalition that revived a dormant campaign to tax financial speculation and to distribute some of the proceeds to social and environmental causes. The organizations involved in this networked campaign again stepped back from branding or owning the campaign and formed a stand-alone organization with a familiar ring: the Robin Hood Tax campaign. This intuitive meme traveled through many nations, engaging people to share stories, meet with political representatives and pressure parties to incorporate it in electoral campaigns. In a relatively short time, the idea received endorsements from prominent politicians and public figures and was soon on the agenda of the European Commission. In 2012, the European Parliament supported initiatives by eleven EU member nations agreed to develop their own versions. These cases suggest that innovative models of organizationally enabled "connective action" may be successful in helping ideas travel in society and into government.[20]

Lesson 4: Political Uptake and Institutional Embedding of Ideas and Values

Due largely to the political uptake of market solutions, the privatization of public goods and services, and the resulting limitation of electoral choices, the social contracts between publics and ruling elites in many nations have been shredded. At the time of this writing, trust in parties and governments hovered below 40 percent in most European democracies, and just above 20 percent in the US. This contrasts with political trust levels near 80 percent in the US in the mid 1960s.[21] (Support for government improved sharply during the Covid-19 pandemic, but the economic paths taken following the crisis will determine longer term trends.) As a result of working less well over time, democracy itself is increasingly challenged as a favored form of governance. Polls show a declining faith in democracy among younger generations in Europe and the US. This is likely because several generations of young citizens have grown up in systems called democracies that have not worked well to represent their interests.[22]

The erosion of democratic institutions has speeded up as new forms of "illiberal" democracy and rightwing populism further distract attention from thinking creatively about what it means for societies to continue to prosper within planetary limits. Meanwhile, on the left, social democratic and labor parties have lost their way and seem unable to produce ideas of much appeal to voters. There appears to be something of a revitalization of European Green parties, but it is not clear what vision of change to expect when many Green politicians talk about "Green growth," and in some cases (e.g. in

Germany) have even formed coalitions with parties on the center right. Perhaps voter support for a Green New Deal will motivate the Greens to put more transformative ideas into that package for uptake in elections and governments.

Meanwhile, ideas about markets, limited government, and climate avoidance continue to hold sway in many nations. How could a bizarre system of welfare support for business while socializing individual risk survive the public outrage surrounding the repeated business and political failings of this century? Many scholars have puzzled over this question. In his aptly named book *Never Let a Good Crisis Go to Waste*, Philip Mirowski pointed to the absence of credible alternatives coming from credible economists, which helps reinforce the conventional wisdom among journalists, business elites, and mainstream politicians that bailing out the old system was the only way to prevent another great depression.[23] In addition, the lack of a credible economic alternative coming from the activist left means that there is no concerted public voice coming from society. This continuing institutionalization of a dysfunctional system is discussed by Colin Crouch in his book *The Strange Non-Death of Neoliberalism,* which outlines the influence of business interests in economic policy, and in politics more generally.[24]

The ironic strengthening of failing state-economy institutions was previewed before the financial crisis by Naomi Klein in her book *The Shock Doctrine: The Rise of Disaster Capitalism.* As briefly discussed earlier, Klein wrote about how national and international governments captured by market and finance interests tend to introduce even harsher market and austerity measures in response to crises created largely by failures of neoliberal policies in the first place. This has happened at the local level, as in the sweeping introduction of charter schools following Hurricane Katrina in New Orleans, as well as in the international arena, such as the radical transformation of ownership, taxes, and trade that put a neoliberal stamp on the chronically dysfunctional startup democracy following the US invasion and occupation of Iraq.[25]

Citizens and movements seeking economic and political change must find ways to transcend the fragmentation that leaves them relatively helpless to challenge the dominant order, even as that establishment loses credibility. As discussed earlier, growing initiatives for a Green New Deal may be promising, but only if civil-society organizations, party leaders, and political funders can imagine a different set of economic principles to put in that package and find better ways to communicate about it. With the growing signs of economic stagnation, and the impact of the Covid-19 pandemic on a fragile global economy, opportunities for change seem present.

Lesson 5: Taking Advantage of Political Opportunities

Those who study social movements often talk about the importance of "political opportunity structures" that signal weakness in an old regime and openings for those promoting new agendas for change. Doug McAdam has outlined four dimensions along which political systems can be analyzed in terms of opportunities for change: (1) the openness of political institutions, (2) the stability of elite alignments, (3) the presence of elite allies of the movement, and (4) levels of state repression against those promoting change.[26] These ideas have been developed and deepened by Sidney Tarrow and Charles Tilly, and in their collaborations with McAdam.[27]

By these measures, many democracies are ripe for change. Thus far, however, the main movements to take advantage of these opportunities are on the far right. Indeed, the openness of political institutions such as parties and elections (opportunity 1 above) has combined with weakness in old elite-party alignments (opportunity 2) to propel many radical right parties into parliaments and governments. Those illiberal movements have met with success in electing parties to represent them, putting allies in parliaments and governments (creating opportunity 3). In more advanced cases such as Hungary, rightwing governments have cracked down on progressive civil-society organizations (opportunity 4 above). When in power, those regimes have doubled down on business deregulation, expanded crony capitalism, rolled back environmental regulations, and promoted other policies that fuel the climate crisis.

However, as noted in Chapter 3, many of these regimes are weak and vulnerable to alternative ideas if they can be developed. The rise of the radical right often introduces strange hybrid forms of economic and political discourses. For example, a number of nations have witnessed a kind of Frankenstein economics that blends various parts of crony capitalism, austerity, welfare nationalism, and Trumpian promises to clean up corruption, which often means introducing new forms of it. It seems that a clear opportunity exists as the early neoliberal funders of some of the radical right networks begin to sense that they have lost control of them, and that they have lost some political influence as a result. For example, after the rise of Trump in 2016, an official of the Koch network admitted they had created a monster they could not control:

> "We are partly responsible," said one former network staffer. "We invested a lot in training and arming a grassroots army that was not controllable, and some of these people have used it in ways that are not consistent with our principles, with our goal of advancing a free society, and instead they have furthered the alt-right …
>
> What we feel really badly about is that we were not able to educate many in the tea party more about how the process works and how free markets work," said the donor. "Seeing this movement that we were part of creating going off in a direction that's anti-free-market, anti-trade, and anti-immigrant – many of us are really saddened by that. Unfortunately, there is little in the short term we can do about that."[28]

Despite their political challenges, unholy alliances between neoliberals and the ethnic nationalist radical right are likely to continue because neoliberals cannot win on the merits of their own ideas, and the populist movements and parties keep the focus on distracting and disruptive symbolic issues, while resisting progressive economic or environmental change. For example, anti-immigrant and racial issues helped drive the Brexit vote in 2016 in the UK and played an important role in the Trump election the same year in the US. In addition, promises to drain the swamp of political corruption aided the elections of Trump, as well as Bolsonaro in Brazil, who quickly earned the title "Tropical Trump" from critics. Despite their scary implications for society, economics, and democracy, the inherent instability of such Frankenstein regimes continues to provide opportunities for progressives to exploit if they can organize more effectively.

Consider the odd forces on the right that led to what might be called a Zombie government under Bolsonaro. Similar to Trump in the US, the Brazilian leader thrived on deception and disinformation in public performances, while shifting the nation's international relationships, and launching a regime of crony capitalism that speeded up environmental exploitation. The election of Bolosnaro, like that of Trump, was widely considered unlikely, but both benefitted from odd assemblages of neoliberal organizations and radical right movements that they tapped into with remarkable skill.

Key elements of the movements that ended up voting for both Trump and Bolsonaro were funded and trained by neoliberal Koch organizations with the aim of disrupting traditional politics. The Koch connection to the Tea Party has been discussed above and is already well known. However, the less publicized Brazil case offers interesting parallels. According to Brazil expert Danniel Gobbi, in the decade before Bolsonaro's election, international free-market libertarian organizations helped create a rightwing libertarian student movement. Support came from several Koch-affiliated organizations in the US, including the Charles Koch Institute, the Cato Institute and the Donors Trust. Additional support was delivered through international affiliates from the neoliberal Atlas Network. Student leaders began training as early as 2007 in the Koch Summer Fellow Program. A national organization called Students for Liberty was formed, and soon expanded with continuing funding for conferences and political training. This group helped form an umbrella network that coordinated national protests under the banner of the Free Brazil Movement.[29] That movement provided some of the popular support base for the impeachment of Brazilian President Dilma Rousseff, in part due to the multi-billion-dollar corruption scandal under her watch involving the Brazilian oil company Petrobras.[30]

Bolsonaro, like Trump, simply entered an existing political party and rode it to victory. Due to conflicts with that party, Bolsonaro later formed his own party, the Alliance for Brazil, which aimed to restore Christian values, and fight against "communism, globalism and any ideology that is against the natural order."[31] Lost in the fog of these chaotic politics was the disruption of the national oil company in the aftermath of the Rousseff scandal, opening possible advantages to Koch energy interests in Brazil. Even if Bolsonaro, like Trump, was not a Koch-groomed candidate, some of the outcomes were compatible with the Koch program of economic anarchy and environmental exploitation.[32] For example, after his election, Bolsonaro soon launched initiatives to sell off oil fields and to privatize Petrobras.

Similar to Trump in the US, this pattern of economic and environmental chaos was aided by a high volume of disinformation and distraction. For example, Bolsonaro appointed to his cabinet a foreign minister who dismissed science as "dogma," and decried the "criminalization" of red meat, oil, and heterosexual sex. As noted in Chapter 1, he also branded climate change as a plot by "criminal Marxists" to "stifle Western economies and promote the growth of China."[33] Perhaps Brazil's foreign minister was a Twitter follower of Donald Trump, who had long before announced the Chinese climate-change hoax when he Tweeted: "The concept of global warming was created by and for the Chinese to make US manufacturing noncompetitive."[34] Trump continued spouting the charge that climate change was a Chinese hoax after becoming president, which provoked an official response from the Chinese foreign minister, who pointed out that Republican presidents Reagan and Bush supported the founding of the United Nations Intergovernmental Panel on Climate Change in the 1980s. The IPCC won the Nobel Prize in 2007 for its work toward "an ever-broader informed consensus about the connection between human activities and global warming."[35]

Behind the theater of the absurd, denying climate change was a convenient cover for the Bolsonaro government to accelerate clearing the Amazon rainforest for agribusiness interests to grow more cattle and soybeans. In the process, indigenous people were displaced, and environmentalists warned about the collapse of this core part of the Earth's ecosystem. When confronted with data from his own government showing Brazil in violation of its commitment in the Paris climate agreement to slow the deforestation, Bolsonaro dismissed the official data as lies. He then fired the director and censored the reports of the government agency responsible for monitoring the Amazon. When the northeast coast suffered a massive oil spill, the environmental minister blamed it on Greenpeace, and Bolsonaro termed it an act of terrorism. Beyond this, he also pressed economic agencies to change data on growth and unemployment, leading international banking institutions to question official government economic data.

Meanwhile, in the US, Donald Trump was also pulling America out of the Paris climate agreement. He also pledged to end what he called "the war on coal." His program of environmental exploitation for short-term corporate gain also included appointing a former coal industry lobbyist as director of the Environmental Protection Agency. Among the many rollbacks were lowered air and water quality standards, and automobile fuel economy and emissions requirements. Following these and dozens of other moves, Trump then gave a speech on "America's environmental leadership" in which he proclaimed his responsible stewardship of public lands, reduction of carbon emissions, and delivery of the "cleanest air" and "crystal clean" water.[36]

As the cases of Brazil and the US suggest, the efforts of radical right movements to seize state power do not always follow a neat blueprint. Indeed, alarming levels of chaos and risk often rise behind the veils of nationalist rhetoric, with results that are seldom good for environment, economy, or society. At the same time, many of these turbulent alignments fail to result in stable regimes. There are, of course, exceptions, as in the illiberal governments in Hungary, Turkey, or Poland, which have sealed themselves against challengers by resorting to state repression of various sorts (see opportunity structure 4 above). As long as democracies like Brazil or the US still have viable electoral, media, and judicial systems, their zombie economic and political regimes present opportunities for challengers. The critical question is: Why is it that in the many nations that display some combination of the first three opportunity structures introduced above, there has been so little gain by movements for progressive change?

Seizing Opportunities for Change

The global economic system today appears ripe for change. Recall from Chapter 3 how an earlier world economic regime proved unmanageable toward the end of the 1960s and provided opportunities for change. The neoliberals were waiting in the wings with ideas that appealed to elite allies and were packaged in attractive ways for voters. There are now many signs that the neoliberal regime is breaking down under inequality, deteriorating state capacities, staggering debt loads, and other problems that are beyond the capacity of most economic models to explain or remedy. The Covid-19 pandemic and its economic aftermath further revealed the precarity of many societies. Yet, where were the alternative ideas positioned for uptake?

The persistence of neoliberal austerity shocks corrupted in many cases by crony capitalism are likely to continue until more coherent alternatives arise. As noted in Chapters 2 and 5, models for sustainable economics have been around for decades, but they continue to sit just beyond the opportunity structures outlined above due to lack of political organization aimed at pressuring elite and party uptake. Without the capacity of movements to engage the opportunities that exist, most centrist business and party elites will continue to prop up a failing system. So far, this might sound like a generic historical plot, except that the contemporary wrinkle involves life as we know it hanging in the balance.

5

Communicating Change: Attention, Amplification, and Organization

As discussed throughout the book, a key reason that nations are having trouble setting and meeting carbon emissions targets and addressing other aspects of the ecological crisis is that most of the approaches focus on the wrong end of the problem. Most national economies remain tied to production, consumption, and transportation models that continue to demand fossil fuels, use high volumes of toxic chemicals, and release the residues into the environment. As a result, demand for dangerous energy sources continues to grow faster than replacement by renewables. And the endless battles to remove one chemical pollutant or clean up another toxic spill are only replaced by the next similar problem.

There are thousands of "wrong end" problems currently competing for attention surrounding the planetary ecological crisis. And there are thousands of organizations fighting different ones of them at different levels of politics around the world. When a particular problem is acute, or an organization hits on a cute or tragic image of an endangered species, media and public attention are momentarily attracted. However, the waves of shifting attention generally fall away again with little overall impact beyond the continued stirring of political conflict with attendant public anger or despair. Since it is impossible to address all of the growing aspects of the ecological crisis at once, the disproportionate amount of attention has been directed at climate change and fossil fuels.

Making global warming and fossil fuels the default problems for the entire crisis turns out to be less than helpful; indeed, their elevation as the poster problems illustrates many of the communication errors introduced in Chapter 1. There are, of course, reasons why we continue to make category mistakes and "wrong-end-of-the-problem" approaches that lead, at best, to marginal adjustments rather than fundamental changes. Among the many reasons why attention is focused on the output rather than input sides of the equation is that "solutions" like carbon taxes or electric cars seem easier to sell to business elites and politicians, who can sell them to publics that they might better spend time educating about deeper solutions. As these patterns become established, many activists and organizations learn that they become recognized as important players when they "become realistic" and embrace those issues, adding more attention to the wrong end of the problem. At that point, the story is now much easier for journalists to tell because: we have the main problem, with a small number of key actors, who provide the points of conflict on which the story turns, and offer reassuring soundbites about solutions, or scary words about the economic costs. In the end, the news turns up the amplifier and directs ever more public attention to limited or outright misguided solutions. There may even be a subliminal reassurance for news consumers that only if these turn out to be the real solutions, we may not have to change how we live after all.

Yet, all the evidence suggests that there will be bigger changes required, and many of them are not at all pleasant if they are born of collapse and growing extinction. What is missing, assuming we want to avoid that scenario, is the capacity to develop appealing images of more resilient and less risky economies that can be adapted to different circumstances. For example, we know that China leads the world in carbon dioxide emissions, along with a host of other toxic problems that are suffered largely by its own population. Much of this is due to becoming the largest industrial engine for consumer demand around the world. Unless patterns of production and consumption change in

Europe, North America, and other prosperous nations, it is not clear what would motivate a top polluter such as China to change its role in the global economy and rethink its own environmental costs. Perhaps a Green New Deal in the US or Europe can focus on more regional and local production, less emphasis on business profits, and more attention to good jobs and social value from public investments. As the world economy de-globalizes, the more prosperous nations also need to rethink foreign aid and development policies. Without such fundamental strategic shifts, the continuing discussions of things like switching to electric cars or transitioning from coal to natural gas may feel good, but in the end, they will not greatly improve the situation.

The moral of this story is that instead of directing attention to misleading versions of problems and solutions, it should be possible to amplify ideas about more vibrant economies that enable different stakeholders and the media to focus attention on more realistic action. This significant change requires improving the flow of ideas among activists, parties, businesses, publics, political funders, and governments to create the support and political will for policies such as: investing in health, education, housing, and other basic social services; discouraging unproductive financial speculation; rebranding consumerism away from the current throwaway mentality toward durability; developing more regional and local production; changing tax structures to reduce inequality and better distribute economic outcomes; shifting development initiatives to promote more self-sufficient economies in poorer nations; and finding ways to reform parties and electoral processes to engage with these issues and better represent the public interest.

These kinds of policies are, of course, contested because business and investors have become so politically dominant and have access to media and publicity channels to spread fear and uncertainty about change. However, there are hopeful signs that environmental crises are getting the attention of business and political leaders who begin to understand the rising costs of doing business as usual. Investments and government subsidies for fossil fuels are being phased out. The World Economic Forum has begun to discuss topics such as the relationship between economy and environment, and problems of inequality. The European Union is discussing how to build a "circular economy." And visions of a Green New Deal are spreading among center-left parties and political factions in the US and Europe.

Making Sure the Contents Suit the Packaging

It is understandable why many activists criticize Green New Deal initiatives as "Greenwashing" – appealing packaging filled with empty ideas. If left to business and political elites to work out, those criticisms will, of course, prove true. However, responsibility falls on citizens and civil-society organizations to develop more unified movements with more compelling communication to mobilize publics and extend their networks to include political parties that can engage voters. Unless better ideas become connected to the political and governmental networks shaping policies, the current opportunities for change will be ground down by business lobbying and "realistic" politicians who are afraid to sell bold ideas to publics who require being educated and led.

Until these things happen, there will be reason to doubt the promises of Green new deals and circular economies. For example, early talk of a Green New Deal emerged from United Nations initiatives following the financial crash of 2008. Kate Raworth observed that many world leaders embraced it and offered hopeful messages of change. But nearly everywhere the idea of growth was baked into thinking about more sustainable recovery: "Angela Merkel suggested 'sustained growth,' David Cameron proposed 'balanced growth,' Barack Obama favored 'long-term, lasting growth,' Europe's José Manuel Barroso was backing 'smart, sustainable, inclusive, resilient growth.' The World Bank promised 'inclusive Green growth'. Other flavors on offer? Perhaps you'd like it to be equitable, good, Greener, low-carbon, responsible or strong. You choose – just so long as you choose growth."[1]

Although Raworth laments how ingrained our thinking about growth has become, she suggests that we avoid direct battles over that idea in the early stages of thinking more creatively about meaningful change. Not only are the growth critics and the fledgling degrowth movement greatly outmatched politically, but publics will require hearing more positive images of economic alternatives before directly confronting problems of growth. Moreover, we know relatively little about what growth will actually look like in economies that adopt different economic models. The variation of regional and national alternatives is likely to be great, particularly among poorer nations. Finally, starting the conversation with growth is again looking at the wrong end of the problem. Growth may be the enemy of sustainability for many reasons, but it is also a symptom of ingrained economic practices that must be reconsidered first, before somehow pulling the plug on growth.

Instead of fighting losing battles over hegemonic ideas like growth, perhaps we should think, instead, about what kind of economies we want to live with and let growth sort itself out amid emerging new realities. Some of Raworth's ideas on sidestepping the growth debate with more positive and easily personalized lifestyle language can be found in her critique of the idea of "degrowth."[2] A response from Giorgos Kallis, a leading degrowth proponent, reveals his ideological commitment to the term because it is incorruptible, and serves as "a missile" in political debates.[3] Such thinking persists, despite its self-limiting networking potential, and dim prospects for interfacing with power. An important question for us all is whether we want to cling to our moralistic or ideological beliefs, even when they are self-limiting, or whether there are better ways to make change? There are many good ideas flowing in degrowth circles but putting them in the current packaging seems to trade political uptake for moral superiority.

Shifting Attention to (Simpler) Ideas about Economic Change

As noted above, global warming has become such a focal issue that it also has become a limitation. It is important to begin telling people that although warming may be the most pressing problem, there are many other issues that threaten life on the planet, and all of them will continue growing worse until more positive alternatives to current economic models are developed and widely shared.

Consider how quickly communication becomes overly complicated if we drill into just one of the many other symptomatic problems of the crisis of ecological economics: the shrinking supplies of fresh water. Despite droughts, melting glaciers, and water table depletion, current industrial practices continue to use and contaminate huge volumes of this precious life stuff in the production of food, fashion, chemicals, and the extraction of raw materials for those and other industries. Just growing the cotton for one t-shirt may consume 700 gallons of water. That is not added to the price of the product because governments often grant free or cheap access to public water supplies in order to attract industries and accommodate their demands. Nor does the price of cheap fashion include the damage from the pesticides used in cotton production, including the long lists of illnesses and deaths in cotton communities.

Even the almond industry turns out to be dangerous in ways not directly connected to global warming. The central valley of California produces the majority of world almonds. The volume of water required for those tasty nuts is hard to fathom in a state prone to drought and growing population needs. It takes about a gallon of water to produce a single almond, and many hundreds of gallons (estimates vary from a few hundred to a thousand) to produce a gallon of almond milk. The annual crop consumes three times the water as the entire city of Los Angeles. Almond producers complain that they are being unfairly singled out, and that they are taking measures to conserve. While we might tell a similar story about industrial meat production (cow milk is even more water intensive), the almond story is worth continuing because it does not end with water. Similar to cotton and many other industrial crops, the toxics used in growing almonds and other agricultural products in the state's main agricultural region have created other ecological crises such as killing off local bee populations. The continuation of this dysfunctional system requires bees to be trucked from across the country to pollinate the annual crop, often leaving the migrant bee colonies woozy and sick as a result. And then there are the health crises being suffered by agricultural workers, which lead to a different set of compartmentalized issues and political conflicts.

Even though these examples of t-shirts and almonds started out being about water, it is hard to talk about them without mentioning the other environmental stress factors involved. For reasons discussed at the beginning of the book, it turns out to be difficult to separate single factors (energy, water, toxics) involved in these systems of production, distribution, consumption, and waste, that have evolved with little overall attention to their human or environmental logic. Separating energy use from toxic chemicals, or chemicals from water use, reflects the narrow category logic of interest politics that many environmentalists, journalists, and politicians have adopted, as discussed in Chapter 2. Perhaps it is time to move away from the limitations of single-issue politics, and the related narrow (mis)categorizations of environmental problems.

Unfortunately, these language and category games often take on lives of their own because they appeal psychologically to politicians, business leaders, political funders, and publics who currently lack the political communication perspectives and processes required to address deeper issues. Moreover, they fragment larger economic problems into separate narrow public policy problems that seldom threaten business as usual. Until various stakeholders change the production, packaging, networking, and uptake of ideas about how to live better with nature, we will continue to suffer communication and politics that focus on the multiplying outputs of dysfunctional economies.

With these communication dilemmas in mind, let's return to the continuing debates over quitting fossil fuels. In addition to the fragmented thinking about the problem, the underlying communication logic begs the large question of what will happen to the economy even if we succeed in pulling out large pieces of such a complex system? What if ending fossil fuels (which won't happen the way we are going about it) would result in an economic crash because the current system cannot function without them? For these and other reasons, the idea of fixing our environmental problems at the output end resembles throwing a wrench into a running engine just because we cannot find the control switch. While throwing a wrench into the works might stop the engine, it is likely to seize up the parts of the motor in unimaginable ways that could prevent it from starting again any time soon.

The point is that even if carbon emissions could be reduced dramatically, it is not clear what effects that would have on underlying economic processes. Those processes are not neutral to the kind of energy they run on, unless the replacements are other, somewhat less damaging, fossil fuels, which doesn't solve the problem. Yet, we regularly hear that using less-damaging fuels such as natural gas instead of coal is just an interim solution. But that begs the question of what new practices are going to come along to change the demand picture? Unless we learn to develop and communicate new economic ideas – and help them flow through society, politics, and business – we are consigned to the current piecemeal attempts to fix the outputs of systems for which we have developed few widely shared alternatives. The first step toward more fundamental economic and political ideas is to adopt a mindset to help see where we want to end up and how to get there with broad support and political uptake.

Setting the Stage for Change: A Mindset for Developing Better Ideas

Before concluding with a look at how the idea-flow model can be used to generate more compelling ideas with better chances of political uptake, two simple background perspectives may help. First, if we aim for meaningful changes in government economic policies and related citizen habits, it is important to develop a pragmatic understanding of how change processes – particularly those that emerge from popular movements – generally work politically. Second, rather than start with debates over what particular technical economic models we need to adopt, it is best to start with more general ideas that open popular readiness to hear about more specifics. The best place to begin is with easily visualized ideas about what economies are for and how they can work differently and better.

How Change Happens: Power, People, and Government

It is ironic, and some would say tragic, that at about the same time in the 1980s that a scientific consensus emerged that human industry was threatening the life support on the planet, the sweeping uptake of the neoliberal political economy regime undermined the capacity of many governments to do much about it. Naomi Klein has described this unfortunate power shift away from government regulation and toward runaway business dominance:

> So my mind keeps coming back to the question: what is wrong with us? I think the answer is far more simple than many have led us to believe: we have not done the things that are necessary to lower emissions because those things fundamentally conflict with deregulated capitalism, the reigning ideology for the entire period we have been struggling to find a way out of this crisis. We are stuck because the actions that would give us the best chance of averting catastrophe – and would benefit the vast majority – are extremely threatening to an elite minority that has a stranglehold over our economy, our political process, and most of our major media outlets ... Indeed, governments and scientists began talking seriously about radical cuts to greenhouse gas emissions in 1988, the exact year that marked the dawning of what came to be called "globalization"...
>
> ... the policies that so successfully freed multinational corporations from virtually all constraints also contributed significantly to the underlying cause of global warming – rising greenhouse gas emissions. The numbers are striking: In the 1990s, as the market integration project ramped up, global emissions were going up an average of one percent a year; by the 2000s, with "emerging markets" like China now fully integrated into the world economy, emissions growth had sped up disastrously ...[4]

In her book *This Changes Everything*, from which these observations were drawn, Klein outlined a compelling case for how our current form of deregulated capitalism has become directly threatening to planetary life-support systems. She calls for the organization of an environmental movement with a more authoritative moral voice.[5] While her analysis has gained broad global recognition, it has also been criticized by critics in the center as too extreme to sell to general publics, and by more radical activists as not being ideologically correct enough. For example, Elizabeth Kolbert reviewed *This Changes Everything* and criticized Klein for being unrealistic in calling for carbon emissions reductions that would seriously alter lifestyles in the prosperous north, saying about the public: "when you tell them what it would take to radically alter carbon emissions, they will turn away."[6] In many ways, Kolbert should be a sympathetic reviewer, given her award winning reporting in the *New York Times* and *New Yorker* on science, environment, and climate change, including a book on the sixth great species extinction currently in progress. However, it seems less than helpful (or fair) to criticize Klein on grounds that it is just not realistic to tell people the truth. Kolbert is undoubtedly correct that people will not clamor for change if they are just given harsh news about the need for personal sacrifices from book authors. However, that is not what Klein was trying to do. She did not suggest that we start with scaring people about their post carbon lifestyles. Her book called for movements to mobilize behind more compelling visions of change. The open question of course is just how to organize such movements so their ideas may gain greater political uptake.

The process of constructing new social realities is often slow and bumpy, but it has happened many times in history. Chapter 3 explained how the currently dysfunctional political economy resulted from political strategies developed over many decades by a well-coordinated movement of elites. As also suggested in that chapter, current critics can learn a great deal from studying how that movement gained such success. Those seeking to change that system will, of course, need to adapt something like the idea-flow model to work under conditions of fewer resources, larger numbers of more diverse organizations, and the commitment to more transparent communication. The focus of this chapter is on how to better coordinate and construct alternative visions under those conditions. The good news is that we do not need to invent new ideas. Many others have already produced great ideas about what economies should really be for, and how they can work better for different people and places. Those ideas just need to become amplified from more sites of production and networked more widely.

A Place to Start: What's the Economy For?

John DeGraf and David Batker wrote a fine book with the arresting title, *What's the Economy For, Anyway?* Their answer is that economies should provide for the greatest good for the greatest number of people, over the longest time. This, of course, means living within the limits of the natural environment. In sketching how this might work they review the many decades of thinking about circular or steady state economics that manage resources and wastes within environmental limits, while prioritizing basic human needs.[7]

The literature on alternative economics is rich and large. Rather than review it all here, it makes more sense to just provide a flavor of what kinds of ideas would meaningfully fill packages such as the Green New Deal or initiatives such as the EU Circular Economy. Few arguments for a better future have combined both the high-level vision and the practical policy proposals found in the report *Prosperity Without Growth* authored by Tim Jackson.[8] That report was published in 2009 by the UK Sustainable Development Commission which was set up by the Labour Government in 2000 and closed by the Conservative-led coalition in 2011. Jackson was the Economics Commissioner for that body and wrote the report based on his experience on the commission and his own work as an ecological economist. The first edition of the report became a modern classic after it was released for free public download by the commission. It has been translated into seventeen languages and was updated in a second edition in 2017.[9] So these ideas are off to a good start.

Jackson offers an inspiring vision explaining how individuals and societies can prosper by finding alternatives to current economic policies and practices. He explains why the factors currently driving economic growth (and how we measure it) have little to do with prosperity. He also suggests a number of simple ways that governments, academics, and citizens can make the idea of a Green New Deal work through gradual economic policy transitions rather than drastic upheaval. These steps include:

- build a macroeconomics for sustainability that can be taught in economics departments and used by economists working for governments
- this ecological economics would include replacing GDP with better measures of prosperity
- focus investment on social wellbeing, by creating more jobs in education, health, childcare, energy, and transportation, along with improving public spaces, facilities, and infrastructure
- tax disruptive financial speculation and other unproductive economic activities
- design taxes and other incentives to increase savings and discourage debt driven consumption
- develop labor and employment policies that strike a better work-life balance
- reduce social and economic inequality with tax, education and social policies
- experiment with ways in which people in different societies can flourish in less stressful economies
- strengthen social capital through community support initiatives
- advertise alternative images of human success and satisfaction beyond wealth accumulation and consumerism
- promote ecological and social values in public communication and education
- monitor and cap resource use and harmful emissions
- change economic and development policies that affect poorer nations by using technology transfer and financial assistance to help poorer nations achieve more economic self-sufficiency with less environmental damage[10]

Such ideas can be adapted by governments in different societies and at different levels from local to international. Indeed, many of these steps toward sustainable prosperity are already appearing in various places. However, we are still lacking a political model to get such ideas out of books and into more widespread circulation and political uptake.

Making the Idea-Flow Model Work

As the above ideas suggest, we should not fear a future based on economic models other than the ones currently being used to drive us to the brink. Nor do we need to think that change must be abrupt or inevitably disruptive, although it is likely to be both if we stay on the current path. Indeed, if rationality prevailed, people would worry far more about continuing to prop up currently dysfunctional economies that are already producing great disruptions.[11] The idea-flow model offers flexible guidelines for how diverse organizations better align around ideas like the ones above that promise more coordinated and effective political action. Consider some ways in which activists, advocacy organizations, think tanks, parties, businesses, concerned citizens, and other stakeholders can increase their political capacity to create change.

Improving Idea Production

Recall from Chapter 3 the breakthrough insight of the early neoliberal movement that ideas can be produced with greater efficiency, coordination, and distribution via think tanks and academic disciplines – set in tune by funders. It is unlikely that current constellations of civil-society organizations will ever attain the level of production efficiency as the Atlas Network of think tanks and its many aligned political organizations, nor is that even desirable. Indeed, such coordination resembles a propaganda system that neither suits essential values of adaptive learning, nor the complexity of our current problems. However, it is surely possible to improve on the currently fragmented state of the many small and struggling progressive think tanks and political organizations. The current sites of idea production can become better coordinated if (a) civil-society organizations relax their ideological, ego, and mission differences, with the help of (b) funders that encourage better alignment by improving the scattered funding models described in the last chapter. The general aim is to bridge differences with ideas that intersect politically, economically, and environmentally and offer adaptive potential in different settings.

The good news is that there are hundreds of organizations exploring new economic ideas around the world, and many more environmental and political organizations that could amplify promising ideas if they are produced with greater clarity and more attractive packaging. Consider just a partial list of current think tanks and academic associations in Europe and North America that are engaged in the production of ideas about ecological economics, and that could develop much better coordination to achieve higher visibility among different movement sectors, publics, politicians, and media:[12]

Institute for Advanced Sustainability Studies, Potsdam Germany
Stockholm Resilience Center
Wellbeing Economy Alliance (WEALL)
Center for the Advancement of the Steady State Economy
New Economy Coalition (NEC)
The Next System Project
Sustainable Consumption Research and Action Initiative
One Earth
Degrow US
Research & Degrowth
New Economics Foundation
Front Porch Republic
Club of Rome
European Economists for an Alternative Economic Policy in Europe
Post-growth Economics Network
Institute for Future Fit Economics
Institute for New Economic Thinking
Institute for Sustainable Communication
Center for Sustainable Economy
The Balaton Group
Future Earth

This list is not intended to be exhaustive or geographically distributed. And it does not include name-brand environment organizations such as 350.org or Greenpeace that have already made efforts to bridge economics and politics (insofar as their charitable status allows). Similarly, there are many multi-issue NGOs such as Oxfam that have demonstrated openness to the kind of networking that amplifies broader agendas. Many of these organizations explicitly call for changes in economic practices to promote better alignment between economies, social needs, and environmental security. Some already have their own networks (e.g. the Wellbeing Economy Alliance has a global network, and the New Economy Coalition has a network of affiliated organizations in the US), but those partners often have their own missions, and lack the resources or incentives to develop common agendas or take concerted action.

Current obstacles to more coordinated idea production include egos, ideologies, fixed organizational missions, and dependence on funders with agendas that limit coordination. A next level of challenge involves the proliferation of idiosyncratic organizational communication models that range over: writing reports of varying density and accessibility, convening stakeholder gatherings, running thematic campaigns on narrow issues, and framing a rainbow of issue messages for particular publics. The mix of different missions with different communication models often blocks convergence of thought and action.

The urgency of the current situation may help diverse organizations seek greater cooperation and coordination in the production of ideas. For example, over 200 experts from civil-society organizations and universities have called for a European Sustainability and Wellbeing Pact.[13] This call to action was circulated in some sixteen languages and in a petition to the EU that quickly received 90,000 signatures. High levels of coordinated input have also gone into the European Union Circular Economy Action Plan, which suggests how governments can promote more idea convergence for programmatic action. Such cooperation in idea production will be most effective when organizations invited to offer advice reach greater agreement on general visions for change. The next challenge is to design packaging to help deliver those ideas to diverse stakeholder networks that engage decisionmakers.

Idea Packaging

As explained in Chapter 3, the neoliberal movement packaged their ideas around a pragmatic but deceptive doctrine of a "double truth." The underlying utopian vision held by movement idealists involved the assumption that markets are the only truly knowledgeable decision-making mechanisms, and that governments must give up efforts to regulate and control them. That inner truth (which turned out to be not true, at least as it has played out empirically) was surrounded by a number of corollaries such as the radical abandonment of social welfare and shifting risk and responsibility to individuals. Those core neoliberal truths and their many social consequences, from homelessness to growing inequality, are hard to sell directly in democracies. As a result, neoliberalism became packaged for popular audiences around promises of greater personal and consumer freedom, mixed with propaganda about the virtues of business and the perils of government incompetence.

Better economic models do not require such deceptive packaging, but they require flexible formats that invite engagement from diverse audiences. It has become common to hear that we need to tell better stories. But what makes for the kind of stories that actors in different networks can identify with, modify, and share? In his presidential address to the American Economic Association, Nobel Laureate Robert Schiller talked about economic narratives and what makes them popular.[14] Although he is critical of many popular economic narratives as corruptions of more powerful mainstream economic theories, he also recognizes that economic stories circulate in society more readily than abstract theories because they include a number of important packaging elements. According to Shiller, effective stories:

- balance emotion and reason
- locate individuals in society through action scenarios (buy, sell, panic, cut taxes, reduce welfare benefits, reducc

inequality, create more socially productive jobs, make business responsible to more diverse stakeholders)
- are amplified by different authorities and influencers that resonate with particular networks
- offer mechanisms for audience feedback
- can be packaged in versions for longer and shorter attention spans
- echo familiar historical and cultural ideas so that they seem approachable.

Variations on these packaging guidelines can be found in many examples of successful communication. For example, in 2007 Annie Leonard (later Executive Director of Greenpeace USA) launched a video that went viral. It was called the *Story of Stuff*. The plot talked about the ways in which consumerism and resource waste have become baked into society and politics and what different visions might look like. The success of that video inspired the *Story of Stuff Project*, which has released a number of other videos that follow a set of packaging principles that locate individuals in communities of action that offer positive solutions.[15]

In these and other discussions, there is agreement that sounding general alarms and then pointing to tired and ineffective solutions is bad packaging. There is also agreement that we should stop blaming individuals (e.g. as consumers) for our problems. The focus is better placed on misguided business policies, or on technology companies with their behavior modification algorithms that saturate the online media environment to make wasteful consumerism the hegemonic idea of our time. This means that instead of promoting solutions through individual actions, successful stories of change start with people and organizations imagining how to change the game, and then developing strategies to pressurize governments to adopt new political goals and policies. These and other tools for idea packaging are presented in short movies called "Story of Change" and "The Story of Solutions."[16] Other videos in the series are called "Story of Electronics," "Story of Cosmetics," "Story of Bottled Water," "Story of Cap and Trade," and "The Story of Water."

Networking Ideas for Change

We have learned from research on ideas that flow over multiple networks that different communication communities often draw different elements from the same packages. Complex ideas should be made easy to take apart so that different elements can spread in particular networks. Labor unions may look for different things from those environmental groups do. This means that idea packages that focus only on the environment and do not talk about jobs and equity will not travel very well in labor networks. Creative idea packaging can help working people imagine living with greater security, better health, secure jobs, more free time, universal education, healthy children, and a better distribution of economic surplus (e.g. profits) in order to accommodate living within limits.

Similarly, new economic and environmental ideas must aim for business support. It turns out that many business sectors are open to better environmental standards, and the business impacts of growing inequalities have emerged as topics at World Economic Forum meetings. Trends in both progressive business networks and some governments indicate a broadening of stakeholder responsibilities to include communities, workers, and environment. Tax policies for creating flexible work and compensating jobs lost to automation may appeal to corporations. There has also been a revival of interest in cooperative worker managed businesses that are attractive in many communities. Some of the organizations and networks listed earlier have developed ideas about that.

Finally, all of these ideas can to be translated into coherent talking points for politicians who need to address a mix of business, labor, and voters about things like business models, tax structures, jobs, and smooth transitions. For political purposes, all of these themes can be reassembled in terms of a bigger package called something like the Green New Deal, or the Circular Economy. The trick is to figure out how different but related ideas inside those packages can be accessed and spread across diverse networks.

Political Uptake

If more coordinated idea networks succeed in spreading new ways to run our economies, they will reach different stakeholders who present demands and opportunities for politicians and parties interested in finding agendas that help get them elected. The neoliberal era transformed most traditional parties, including many on the center left, into intellectually hollow marketing operations dedicated mainly to winning elections, protecting their share of state resources, and positioning themselves as attractive coalition partners. However, there are signs of resurgence among European Green parties that may provide political leverage. In the US, public interest business initiatives may grow with policy incentives from progressive states.

This era of cartel parties and post-democracy has not been an easy one for enacting either economic or environmental reforms. However, the scale of both environmental and economic problems may prompt a time of political renewal and realignment. Of course, the instability may also push parties and elections the other way, with authoritarian politicians who limit the capacity of democracies to represent the public interest in these crucial areas. These unfortunate scenarios emerged in Brazil with Bolsonaro, India under Modi, and the US with Trump. Whether the direction is toward democratic renewal or continuing erosion depends, in part, on developing capacities for more coordinated idea production, packaging clearer visions, sharing them across diverse stakeholder networks, and including opportunistic politicians in those networks.

Conclusion

If we want to communicate and act more effectively on our many environmental crises, we need to start thinking differently – now – about economics and politics. One simple step discussed in Chapter 1 is to learn that how we categorize problems affects how we approach solutions, and how effective those solutions are. It is increasingly clear that as long as we categorize the growing numbers of environmental crises as separate symptomatic environmental problems, rather than as common products of the current economic system, there will continue to be little progress.

The next helpful move is to learn to communicate at the intersection of environment, economy, and politics. Elements from all three areas are involved in defining problems and finding more effective solutions. Movements with messages that include environment, economy, and democracy are likely to get more attention and uptake from parties and politicians who learn that they can better talk to voters about security, sustainability, and wellbeing – values which ought to be at the heart of any viable economy. Attractive policies that reflect these values can be packaged as part of a "Green New Deal" that includes such elements as: better distribution of economic outputs; striking a better balance among business interests, social wellbeing, and environmental resilience; reducing the amount of work required for livable wages; slowing down our stressed-out, speeded-up lives; changing how we consume; living with less debt; developing more local production and energy generation; and investing public resources in social projects that build stronger communities. In order to make these things happen, politicians can also tap into growing popular support for reducing current levels of inequality and concentrations of wealth and power.

The problems and solutions facing poorer nations understandably look very different: restoring the capacities of failed and limited states, ending commodity extraction that benefits neither local populations nor nature, and experimenting with local and regional economies that are measured in terms other than GDP. More prosperous nations need to change their trade practices and foreign-aid philosophies, and they must also change postcolonial efforts to continue "development" policies that have largely failed since the end of the colonial era. In addition, significant change will likely require stronger international institutions such as a World Environmental and Economic Organization that might replace the increasingly moribund World Trade Organization that caused so much damage during the peak era of neoliberal globalization.

Much of the focus of this book has been on the more developed industrial and post-industrial nations because they have created most of the problems. And they have the greatest capacity and responsibility for developing solutions. Even within that set of countries, the focus here has been on democracies because they offer greater hopes for change driven by popular movements and ideas. In addition, the democracies have an historical record of cooperation based on similar economies, international political networks, and security arrangements. New ideas that work in one place are likely to travel to others.

In the final analysis, we are all change agents. An important step in becoming more effective is to understand that the deep cultural and political scripts that shape a good deal of our thinking about prosperity have led us badly astray. Reimagining what it means to prosper and thrive are liberating activities both individually and collectively. May we all live long and prosper.

Notes

Introduction: The Future is Now

1 Greta Thunberg, "'You Did Not Act in Time.' Greta Thunberg's Full Speech to MPs," *Guardian*, April 23, 2019. https://www.theguardian.com/environment/2019/apr/23/greta-thunberg-full-speech-to-mps-you-did-not-act-in-time
2 Matthew Taylor, Libby Brooks, and Arthur Nelson, "Youth Climate Strikes Take Place in More than 100 countries," *Guardian*, March 14, 2019. https://www.theguardian.com/education/2019/mar/14/youth-climate-strikes-to-take-place-in-almost-100-countries-greta-thunberg
3 "Environmental Protection vs. Economic Growth," Gallup Poll (2018). https://news.gallup.com/poll/1615/environment.aspx
4 Graeme Maxton and Jorgen Randers. *Reinventing Prosperity: Managing Economic Growth to Reduce Unemployment, Inequality and Climate Change* (Greystone Books, 2016).
5 James K. Galbraith, "The Unsustainability of Inequality," *Project Syndicate*, August 23, 2019. https://www.project-syndicate.org/onpoint/the-unsustainability-of-inequality-by-james-k--galbraith-2019-08?barrier=accesspaylog
6 Ibid.
7 See Guy Standing, *The Precariat: The New Dangerous Class* (London: Bloomsbury, 2014)
8 Adam Corner, "A new Conversation with the Center Right about Climate Change: Values, Frames, and Narratives," Climate Outreach and Information Network, June 13, 2013.

https://e-voice.org.uk/kef/about/view/useful-information/conversing-climate-change.pdf

9 Bill McKibben, "Don't Imagine the Future – It's Already Here," *Organization*, 20 (5), 2013, 745–747.

1 Communicating Complex Problems

1 International Energy Agency, "Global Energy Review 2020: The Impacts of the Covid-19 Crisis on Global Energy Demand and CO2 Emissions," April 2020. https://www.iea.org/reports/global-energy-review-2,011

2 Intergovernmental Panel on Climate Change, "Special Report: Global Warming of 1.5° C," 2018. https://www.ipcc.ch/sr15/

3 George Monbiot, "Airlines and Oil Giants Are on the Brink. No Government Should Offer them a Lifeline," *Guardian*, April 29, 2020. https://www.theguardian.com/commentisfree/2,011/apr/20/airlines-oil-giants-government-economy

4 Jillian Ambrose, "ExxonMobil Tried to Get European Green Deal Watered Down," *Guardian*, March 6, 2020. https://www.theguardian.com/business/2,011/mar/-3/exxonmobil-tried-to-get-european-green-deal-watered-down-claims-climate-lobbying-watchdog

5 Bill McKibben, "Don't Imagine the Future – It's Already Here."

6 Adam Frank, "New Climate Books Stress We Are Already Far Down the Road to a Different Earth," *National Public Radio Book Reviews*, March 25, 2019. https://www.npr.org/2019/03/25/706499110/new-climate-books-stress-we-are-already-far-down-the-road-to-a-different-earth?t=1553622503730&t=1553680631324

7 Cylvia Hayes, "Normal Was Killing Us," *3E Strategies Blog*, April 23, 2020. http://www.3estrategies.org/blog/2,011/-5/14/normal-was-killing-us/

8 Philip Shabecoff, "Global Warming Has Begun, Expert Tells Senate," *New York Times*, June 24, 1988. https://www.nytimes.com/1,979/-3/15/us/global-warmıng-has-begun-expert-tells-senate.html

9 Oliver Milman, "Ex-NASA Scientist: 30 Years ON, World is Failing 'Miserably' to Address Climate

Change," *Guardian*, June 19, 2018. https://www.theguardian.com/environment/2018/jun/19/james-hansen-nasa-scientist-climate-change-warning

10 Murray Edelman, *Political Language: Words that Succeed and Policies that Fail* (New York: Academic Press, 1977).

11 United Nations, Sustainable Development Goals Knowledge Platform, 2015. https://sustainabledevelopment.un.org/post2015/transformingourworld

12 Jason Hickel, "The Contradiction of the Sustainable Development Goals: Growth Versus Ecology on a Sustainable Planet." *Sustainable Development*, 2019, 1–12. doi: 10.1002/sd.1947.

13 Rebecca Lindsey, "Climate Change: Atmospheric Carbon Dioxide," NOAA Climate.gov, August 1, 2018. https://www.climate.gov/news-features/understanding-climate/climate-change-atmospheric-carbon-dioxide

14 Peter Frumhoff, "Global Warming Fact: More than Half of All Industrial CO2 Pollution Has Been Emitted Since 1988," *Union of Concerned Scientists Blog*, December 15, 2014. https://blog.ucsusa.org/peter-frumhoff/global-warming-fact-co2-emissions-since-1988-764

15 John Naish, "Could Dimming the Sun Save the Earth? Bill Gates Wants to Spray Millions of Tonnes of Dust into the Stratosphere to Stop Global Warming ... but Critics Fear It Could Trigger Calamity," *Daily Mail*, August 13, 2019. https://www.dailymail.co.uk/sciencetech/article-7350713/Bill-Gates-wants-spray-millions-tonnes-dust-stratosphere-stop-global-warming.html. See also, Harvard University School of Engineering, "Harvard Project to Address Uncertainties in Solar Geoengineering," July 29, 2019. https://www.seas.harvard.edu/news/2019/07/harvard-project-to-address-uncertainties-in-solar-geoengineering

16 The term "surveillance capitalism" is from Shoshana Zuboff, *The Age of Surveillance Capitalism: The Fight for the Future at the New Frontier of Power* (New York: Public Affairs Books, 2019). Despite her radical critique of how media companies invade our privacy to shape consumer behavior, there is almost no mention of the environmental costs of this warp speed economy.

17 Bill McKibben, "Don't Imagine the Future – It's Already Here," p. 745.

18 Murray Edelman, *Political Language.*

19 Maxwell Boykoff, *Creative (Climate) Communications: Productive Pathways for Science, Policy and Society* (New York, Cambridge University Press, 2019), p. 233, Kindle edn.

20 James Temple, "Our Pathetically Slow Shift to Clean Energy, In Five Charts," *MIT Technology Review*, December 24, 2019. https://www.technologyreview.com/s/614917/our-pathetically-slow-shift-to-clean-energy-in-five-charts/

21 Carine Sebi, "Explaining the Increase of Coal Consumption Worldwide," *The Conversation*, February 24, 2019. https://theconversation.com/explaining-the-increase-in-coal-consumption-worldwide-111045

22 UN News, "Climate Change," July 31, 2019. https://news.un.org/en/story/2019/07/1043551

23 Rebecca Lindsey, "Climate Change: Global Sea Level," National Oceanic and Atmospheric Administration, Climate.gov, November 19, 2019. https://www.climate.gov/news-features/understanding-climate/climate-change-global-sea-level. Joe Romm, "Last Time CO2 Levels Were This High, Sea Levels Were 60 Feet Higher, and Antartica Had Trees," *ThinkProgress*, April 8, 2019. https://thinkprogress.org/carbon-dioxide-levels-sea-antarctica-b435497e1266/

24 Murray Edelman, *The Symbolic Uses of Politics* (Urbana, IL: University of Illinois Press, 1964).

25 John Lanchester, "Two New Books Dramatically Capture the Climate Change Crisis," *New York Times Book Review*, April 12, 2019. https://www.nytimes.com/2019/04/12/books/review/david-wallace-wells-uninhabitable-earth-nathaniel-rich-losing-earth.html

26 Bill Gates, "My Favorite Book of All Time," *The Blog of Bill Gates,* January 26, 2018. https://www.gatesnotes.com/Books/Enlightenment-Now. See Steven Pinker, *Enlightenment Now: The Case for Reason, Science, Humanism and Progress* (New York: Penguin Books, 2018).

27 For a direct criticism of Gates and Pinker, see Jason Hickel, "Bill Gates Says Poverty Is Decreasing. He Couldn't Be More Wrong," *Guardian*, January 29, 2019. https://www.theguardian.com/commentisfree/2019/jan/29/bill-gates-davos-global-poverty-infographic-neoliberal. For a more

data-heavy analysis suggesting that the individual level gains of civilization are unevenly distributed at best: Richard Wilkinson and Kate Pickett, *The Spirit Level: Why Greater Equality Makes Societies Stronger*. Bloomsbury Press, 2009.

28 See George E. Marcus, W. Russell Neuman, and Michael MacKuen, *Affective Intelligence and Political Judgment* (Chicago: University of Chicago Press, 2000).

29 Bill Gates, "Climate Change and the 75% Problem," *The Blog of Bill Gates*, October 17, 2018. https://www.gatesnotes.com/Energy/My-plan-for-fighting-climate-change. See also John Vidal, "How Bill Gates aims to clean up the planet," *Guardian*, February 4, 2018. https://www.gatesnotes.com/Energy/My-plan-for-fighting-climate-change

30 Nafeez Ahmed, "Nasa-Funded Study: Industrial Civilization Headed for 'Irreversible Collapse'?" *Guardian*, March 14, 2014. https://www.theguardian.com/environment/earth-insight/2014/mar/14/nasa-civilisation-irreversible-collapse-study-scientists

31 Justin Lewis, *Beyond Consumer Capitalism: Media and the Limits to Imagination* (Cambridge UK: Polity, 2013).

32 Justin Lewis, "Consumerism and the Limits to Imagination," DVD transcript, 2014. https://www.mediaed.org/transcripts/Consumerism-And-The-Limits-Transcript.pdf

33 Kate Raworth, *Doughnut Economics: Seven Ways to Think Like a 21st-Century Economis*t (Hartford Vermont: Chelsea Green Publishing, 2017).

34 Jay G. Blumler and Dennis Kavanagh. "The Third Age of Political Communication: Influences and Features." *Political Communication* 16.3 (1999): 209–230.

35 Colin Crouch, *Post-Democracy* (Cambridge, UK: Polity, 2004).

36 In Europe, for example, the Eurobarometer poll of citizens in European Union member nations found that in 2018 only 35 percent, on average, trust their national governments. See "Public Opinion in the European Union." Eurobarometer 90, polls conducted November 2018. (Brussels: The European Commission, 2019). http://ec.europa.eu/commfrontoffice/publicopinion/index.cfm

37 W. Lance Bennett, Alexandra Segerberg, and Curd B. Knüpfer. "The Democratic Interface: Technology, Political Organization, and Diverging Patterns of Electoral

Representation," *Information, Communication and Society* 21 (2018): 1655–1680.

38 Manuel Castells, *The Rise of the Network Society*, vol. 1, 2nd edn. (New York: Wiley, 2010).

39 W. Lance Bennett and Alexandra Segerberg, *The Logic of Connective Action: Digital Media and the Personalization of Contentious Politics* (New York: Cambridge University Press, 2014).

40 W. Lance Bennett, Alexandra Segerberg, and Yunkang Yang. "The Strength of Peripheral Networks: Negotiating Attention and Meaning in Complex Media Ecologies." *Journal of Communication* 68.4 (2018): 659–684.

41 See David Karpf, *Analytic Activism: Digital Listening and the New Political Strategy* (New York: Oxford University Press, 2016).

42 Bruce Bimber, Andrew Flanagin, and Cynthia Stohl, *Collective Action in Organizations: Interaction and Engagement in an Era of Technological Change* (New York Cambridge University Press, 2012).

43 Bennett and Segerberg, *The Logic of Connective Action*, chs. 1 and 4.

44 Alex Pentland, *Social Physics: How Networks Can Make Us Smarter* (New York: Penguin Books, 2014).

45 See: https://www.atlasnetwork.org/about/our-story. Also: https://www.atlasnetwork.org/partners/global-directory

46 See Fridays For Future website: https://www.fridaysforfuture.org/

2 What's Missing in Environmental Communication?

1 Naomi Klein, *The Shock Doctrine: The Rise of Disaster Capitalism* (New York: Henry Holt, 2007).

2 Rachel Carson, *Silent Spring* (Houghton Mifflin, 1962).

3 See the Club of Rome website: https://www.clubofrome.org/activities/reports/

4 An update of this report is published as *The Limits to Growth: The 30-year Update* (Chelsea Green, 2004). A condensed version of the original report is available as:

Donella H. Meadows, Dennis I. Meadows, Jorgen Randers, and William H. Behrens III, *The Limits to Growth: A Report to the Club of Rome*. http://www.ask-force.org/web/Global-Warming/Meadows-Limits-to-Growth-Short-1972.pdf

5 Herman E. Daly, *Steady-State Economics: With New Essays* (Island Press, 1991).

6 See Kate Raworth's website at: https://www.kateraworth.com/doughnut/

7 See the Club of Rome website: https://www.clubofrome.org/activities/reports/

8 Center for the Advancement of the Steady State Economy, "What Is a Steady State Economy?" https://steadystate.org/wp-content/uploads/CASSE_Brief_SSE.pdf

9 Herman E. Daly, *Steady-State Economics*.

10 See, for example: The Global Footprint Network https://www.footprintnetwork.org/about-us/our-history/ and the Center for the Advancement of the Steady State Economy https://steadystate.org/

11 See for example: Bill McKibben, *Deep Economy: The Wealth of Communities and The Durable Future* (New York: Henry Holt, 2007); Rob Dietz and Dan O'Neill, *Enough Is Enough: Building a Sustainable Economy in a World of Finite Resources* (Routledge, 2013); and Kate Raworth, *Doughnut Economics*.

12 The EU Green Ten: https://green10.org/

13 Center for Media and Democracy. *Sourcewatch*. https://www.sourcewatch.org/index.php/WWF

14 Michael Greshko, "Current Climate Pledges Aren't Enough to Stop Severe Warming," *National Geographic*, October 31, 2017. https://news.nationalgeographic.com/1,962/-45/paris-agreement-climate-change-usa-nicaragua-policy-environment/

15 Adlai Stevenson, Speech to the Economic and Social Council of the United Nations, Geneva Switzerland, July 9, 1965.

16 Kenneth E. Boulding, "The Economics of Coming Spaceship Earth," in Henry Jarrett, ed., *Environmental Quality in A Growing Economy* (Johns Hopkins University Press, 1966), pp. 3–14.

17 The reader can easily view these results by going to Google Trends (https://trends.google.com). I chose the following

search comparisons: climate change, Greta Thunberg, global warming. The search period I used was July 25, 2018 – July 25, 2019. I selected worldwide results, although the reader may see how different countries compare.

18 United Nations Environment Programme, "Frontiers 2018/19: Emerging Issues of Environmental Concern," March 4, 2019. https://www.unenvironment.org/resources/frontiers-201,764-emerging-issues-environmental-concern

19 "From DDT to Glyphosate: Rachel Carson We Need You Again," *YouTube* (June 21, 2016) https://www.youtube.com/watch?v=mF2iS5vIamg

20 Evaggelos Vallianatos, "Deleterious Politics: From DDT to Roundup," *Independent Science News*, July 17, 2015. https://www.independentsciencenews.org/environment/ruthless-power-and-deleterious-politics-from-ddt-to-roundup/

21 Martin Breum, "How the Narrative on Polar Bears Has Become a Problem for Arctic Environmental Groups," *Arctic Today*, October 31, 2018. https://www.arctictoday.com/narrative-polar-bears-become-problem-arctic-environmental-groups/

22 Anthony Giddens, *The Politics of Climate Change* (Cambridge, UK: Polity, 2009), p. 50.

23 Anthony Giddens, "Why We Should Ditch the Green Movement," *Guardian*, November 1, 2006. https://www.theguardian.com/commentisfree/2006/nov/01/post561

24 Frank Uekötter, "Entangled Ecologies: Outlines of a Green History of Two or More Germanies," in Frank Bösch, ed., *A History Divided: East and West Germany Since the 1970s* (Berghahn Books, 2018), p. 148.

25 See Bob Strauss, "The Top Ten Wildlife Conservation Organizations," *ThoughtCo.*, July 7, 2019. https://www.thoughtco.com/top-wildlife-conservation-organizations-4088567

26 "Air Pollution: Know Your Enemy," United Nations Environmental Programme, September 10, 2018. https://www.unenvironment.org/news-and-stories/story/air-pollution-know-your-enemy

27 A copy of this report can be found here: https://sustainabledevelopment.un.org/content/documents/5987our-common-future.pdf

28 See Jason Chumtong and David Kaldewey, "Beyond the

Google Ngram Viewer: Bibliographic Databases and Journal Archives as Tools for the Quantitative Analysis of Scientific and Meta-Scientific Concepts," Forum Internationale Wissenschaft, University of Bonn, Working Paper No. 8, 2017. https://www.fiw.uni-bonn.de/publikationen/FIWWorkingPaper/fiw-working-paper-no.-8, 6–8.

29 For a review of more of the converging threads of this idea, see Danny Stofleth, "A Short History of Sustainable Development," *Rethinking Prosperity*, February 23, 2015. http://rethinkingprosperity.org/2015/02/23/

30 Green Party of Ireland, September 25, 2015. https://www.greenparty.ie/greens-un-sustainable-development-goals-are-a-manifesto-for-the-future-of-both-the-global-north-and-south/

31 For an excellent comparison of different patterns of government uptake of the idea of sustainable development, see: Caterina Rost, *The Divergent Trajectories of an Idea: Sustainable Development in Germany and the United States*. Ph.D. dissertation, University of Washington, 2017.

32 German Council for Sustainable Development, "German Almanac of Sustainability: 2017," April 20. https://www.nachhaltigkeitsrat.de/en/german-almanac-of-sustainability/

33 Ibid., pp. 83–122.

34 "Success Stories," United Nations Sustainable Development Goals, 2018. https://www.un.org/sustainabledevelopment/blog/category/hlpf2018/success-stories/

3 Economy vs. Environment: Selling Predatory Economics

1 Eva Friman, *No Limits: The 20th Century Discourse on Economic Growth*. Doctoral Thesis (Umea University, Sweden, 2002).

2 Ibid., pp. 18–19.

3 Shane R. Tomashot, Selling Peace: The History of the International Chamber of Commerce, 1919–1925. Ph.D. dissertation (Georgia State University 2015) p. 30. https://scholarworks.gsu.edu/history_diss/43/

4 Jurgen Reinhoudt and Serge Audier. *The Walter Lippmann*

Colloquium: The Birth of Neo-liberalism (Cham, Switzerland: Palgrave Macmillan/Springer, 2018) p. 7.

5 See the Mont Pelerin Society website: https://www.montpelerin.org/

6 Philip Mirowski, "The Political Movement That Dared Not Speak Its Own Name: The Neoliberal Thought Collective Under Erasure," Institute for New Economic Thinking, Working Paper No. 23 (North Bend, Indiana: Notre Dame University, September 2014) https://www.ineteconomics.org/research/research-papers/the-political-movement-that-dared-not-speak-its-own-name-the-neoliberal-thought-collective-under-erasure

7 Interview with Hayek in the Chilean paper *El Mercurio* during his visit in 1981. Reported by Corey Robin, "The Hayek-Pinochet Connection: A Second Reply to My Critics," *Crooked Timber*, June 25, 2013. http://crookedtimber.org/2013/06/25/the-hayek-pinochet-connection-a-second-reply-to-my-critics/. Other discussions by Hayek on the dangers of democracy and the prospects for authoritarian liberalism can be found in his book *The Constitution of Liberty: The Definitive Edition* (London: Routledge, 2013).

8 George Monbiot, "Neoliberalism – the Ideology at the Root of All Our Problems," *Guardian*, April 15, 2016. https://www.theguardian.com/books/2016/apr/15/neoliberalism-ideology-problem-george-monbiot

9 Ibid.

10 George H. Smith, "Anthony Fisher and the Influence of Intellectuals on Modern Society," *The Atlas Network Newsletter*, June 25, 2015. https://www.atlasnetwork.org/news/article/antony-fisher-and-the-influence-of-intellectuals-on-modern-society

11 Institute of Economic Affairs, Brexit Unit. https://iea.org.uk/category/brexit/

12 https://www.atlasnetwork.org

13 David Harvey, *A Brief History of Neoliberalism* (New York: Oxford University Press, 2007).

14 Richard Fink, "The Structure of Social Change," 1996, p. 3. https://archive.org/stream/TheStructureOfSocialChangeLibertyGuideRichardFinkKoch/The%20Structure%20of%20Social%20Change%20_%20Liberty%

20Guide%20_%20Richard%20Fink%20_%20Koch_djvu.txt

15 Philip Mirowski, "Postface: Defining Neoliberalism," in Philip Mirowski and Dieter Plehwe, eds., *The Road from Mont Pelerin: The Making of the Neoliberal Thought Collective* (Cambridge MA: Harvard University Press, 2009), p. 444.

16 Nancy MacLean, *Democracy in Chains: The Deep History of the Radical Right's Stealth Plan for America* (New York: Penguin, 2017).

17 Charles Koch University Funding Database, Greenpeace, 2017. https://polluterwatch.org/charles-koch-university-funding-database

18 Avner Offer and Gabriel Söderberg. *The Nobel Factor: The Prize in Economics, Social Democracy, and the Market Turn* (Princeton, NJ: Princeton University Press, 2016).

19 Philip Mirowski, "Why Is There a Nobel Memorial Prize in Economics?" August 17, 2011, iNET channel, *YouTube* https://www.youtube.com/watch?v=dLtEo8lplwg

20 The Nobel Prize, https://www.nobelprize.org/prizes/economic-sciences/

21 Agence France Presse, "Nobel Descendant Slams Economics Prize," *The Local (Sweden)*, September 28, 2005. https://www.thelocal.se/20120102/2173

22 International Chamber of Commerce. https://iccwbo.org/about-us/global-network/

23 Felicity Lawrence, Rob Evans, David Pegg, Caelainn Barr, and Pamela Duncan, "How the Right's Radical Thinktanks Reshaped the Conservative Party," *Guardian*, November 29, 2019. https://www.theguardian.com/politics/2019/nov/29/rightwing-thinktank-conservative-boris-johnson-brexit-atlas-network

24 Jane Mayer, *Dark Money: The Hidden History of the Billionaires Behind the Rise of the Radical Right* (New York: Doubleday, 2016).

25 Stephen Metcalf, "Neoliberalism: The Idea that Swallowed the World," *Guardian*, August 18, 2017. https://www.theguardian.com/news/2017/aug/18/neoliberalism-the-idea-that-changed-the-world

26 Felicity Lawrence, et al., "How the Radical Right's Thinktanks Reshaped the Conservative Party."

27 Joseph Stiglitz, "The End of Neo-liberalism?" *Project Syndicate,* July 7, 2008. https://www.project-syndicate.org/commentary/the-end-of-neo-liberalism?barrier=accesspaylog
28 Steve Horn, "Kochtopus Cato Institute Power Grab: A Historical Perspective," *Desmog,* March 7, 2012. https://www.desmogblog.com/kochtopus-cato-institute-power-grab-historical-perspective
29 "The Financial Crisis and the Role of Federal Regulators," House Hearing No 110, House Committee on Oversight and Government Reform, October 23, 2008. https://www.govinfo.gov/content/pkg/CHRG-110hhrg55764/html/CHRG-110hhrg55764.htm
30 James K. Galbraith, "The Next Great Transformation, *Project Syndicate*, November 8, 2019, pp. 4–5. https://www.project-syndicate.org/onpoint/the-next-great-transformation-by-james-k-galbraith-2019-11?barrier=accesspaylog
31 David Harvey, *A Brief History of Neoliberalism*, ch. 3.

4 Democracy with a Future: Mobilizing Ideas and Opportunities for Change

1 Fiona Harvey, Jennifer Rankin, and Daniel Boffey. "European Green Deal Will Change Economy to Solve Climate Crisis, Says EU," *Guardian*, December 11, 2019. https://www.theguardian.com/environment/2019/dec/11/european-green-deal-will-change-economy-to-solve-climate-crisis-says-eu
2 Crouch, *Post-Democracy*.
3 Donatella della Porta, *Can Democracy Be Saved? Participation, Deliberation, and Social Movements* (Cambridge, UK: Polity, 2013).
4 Donatella della Porta, "Multiple Belongings, Tolerant Identities, and the Construction of 'Another Politics': Between the European Social Fora and Local Fora," in Donatella della Porta and Sidney Tarrow, eds., *Transnational Protest and Global Activism* (Lanham, MD: Rowman & Littlefield, 2005), pp. 175–203.
5 See Bennett, Segerberg, and Knüpfer, "The Democratic Interface."
6 Ibid.

7 Alexander Hertel-Fernandez, Theda Scocpol, and Jason Sklar, "When Mega Donors Join Forces: How the Koch Network and the Democracy Alliance Influence Organized US Politics on the Right and Left," *Harvard Scholar*, p. 3. https://scholar.harvard.edu/files/ahertel/files/donorconsortia-named.pdf. A shorter version has been published in *Studies in American Political Development* 32.2 (2018): 127–165.

8 Ibid., p. 36.

9 Ibid., p. 44.

10 Quinn Slobodian, "Democracy Doesn't Matter to the Defenders of 'Economic Freedom,'" *Guardian*, November 11, 2019. https://www.theguardian.com/commentisfree/2019/nov/11/democracy-defenders-economic-freedom-neoliberalism

11 Ida Kubiszewski, "Beyond GDP: Are there Better Ways to Measure Well-Being?" *The Conversation*, December 1, 2014. http://theconversation.com/beyond-gdp-are-there-better-ways-to-measure-well-being-33414

12 United Nations Development Program, "Human Development Report, 2019." http://report.hdr.undp.org/

13 G. R. Steele, "There Is No Such Thing as Society," Institute for Economic Affairs, September 30, 2009. https://iea.org.uk/blog/there-is-no-such-thing-as-society

14 Ronald Reagan, press conference, August 12, 1986. Source: The Reagan Library. https://www.reaganfoundation.org/ronald-reagan/reagan-quotes-speeches/news-conference-1/

15 International Degrowth Web Portal. https://www.degrowth.info/en/what-is-degrowth/

16 Degrowth website: https://www.degrowth.info/en/what-is-degrowth/

17 Kate Raworth, *Doughnut Economics*.

18 David Harvey, *A Brief History of Neoliberalism*; Dieter Plehwe, "Introduction," *The Road from Mont Pelerin: The Making of the Neoliberal Thought Collective*, Philip Mirowski and Dieter Plehwe, eds. (Cambridge MA: Harvard University Press, 2009), pp. 1– 43.

19 See Bennett and Segerberg, *The Logic of Connective Action*.

20 Ibid.

21 Pew Research Center, "Public Trust in Government Near Historic Lows," April 11, 2019. https://www.people-press.org/2019/04/11/public-trust-in-government-1958-2019/

22 Roberto Stefan Foa, and Yascha Mounk, "The Democratic Disconnect." *Journal of Democracy* 27 (2016): 5–17.
23 Philip Mirowski, *Never Let a Good Crisis Go to Waste: How Neoliberalism Survived the Financial Crisis* (London: Verso, 2013).
24 Colin Crouch, *The Strange Non-Death of Neoliberalism* (Cambridge, UK: Polity, 2011).
25 Naomi Klein, *The Shock Doctrine: The Rise of Disaster Capitalism* (New York: Henry Holt, 2007).
26 Doug McAdam, "Conceptual Origins, Current Problems, Future Directions," in Doug McAdam, John D. McCarthy, and Mayer N. Zald, eds., *Comparative perspectives on Social Movements: Political Opportunities, Mobilizing Structures, and Cultural Framings* (New York: Cambridge University Press, 1996), pp. 23–40.
27 See Sidney G. Tarrow, *Power in Movements: Social Movements in Contentious Politics*, 3rd edn. (New York: Cambridge University Press, 2011); and Douglas McAdam, Sidney Tarrow, and Charles Tilly, *Dynamics of Contention* (New York: Cambridge University Press, 2001).
28 Kenneth P. Vogel, "Behind the Retreat of the Koch Brothers' Operation, *Politico*, October 27, 2016. https://www.politico.com/story/2016/10/koch-brothers-campaign-struggles-230325
29 Danniel Gobbi, "Identidade em ambiente virtual: uma análise da Rede Estudantes Pela Liberdade" (unpublished Master Thesis). University of Brasília, Brazil, 2016.
30 Dom Phillips, "Brazil's Right on the Rise as Anger Grows Over Scandal and Corruption," *Guardian*, July 25, 2017. https://www.theguardian.com/world/2017/jul/26/brazil-rightwing-dilma-rousseff-lula
31 *Deutsche Welle*, "Brazil: President Jair Bolsonaro Forms His Own New Political Party," November 22, 2019. https://www.dw.com/en/brazil-president-jair-bolsonaro-forms-his-own-new-political-party/a-51361998
32 Summary of reporting by *Telesur*: "Were the Koch Brothers Behind the Impeachment of Brazil's President Dilma Rousseff?" *Global Research*, May 15, 2016. https://www.globalresearch.ca/are-the-koch-brothers-behind-brazils-anti-dilma-march/5525269
33 Jonathan Watts, "Brazil's New Foreign Minister Believes

Climate Change Is A Marxist Plot," *Guardian*, November 15, 2018. https://www.theguardian.com/world/2018/nov/15/brazil-foreign-minister-ernesto-araujo-climate-change-marxist-plot

34 @realDonaldTrump, November 6, 2012. https://twitter.com/realdonaldtrump/status/265895292191248385?lang=en

35 Tom Phillips, "Climate Change a Chinese Hoax? Beijing Gives Donald Trump a Lesson in History," *Guardian*, November 17, 2016. https://www.theguardian.com/us-news/2016/nov/17/climate-change-a-chinese-plot-beijing-gives-donald-trump-a-history-lesson

36 Katie Rogers and Coral Davenport, "Trump Saw Opportunity in Speech on Environment. Critics Saw A '1984' Moment," *New York Times*, July 8, 2019. https://www.nytimes.com/2019/07/08/us/politics/trump-environment-climate-change.html

5 Communicating Change: Attention, Amplification, and Organization

1 Kate Raworth, *Doughnut Economics,* ch. 1, p. 35 e-book edn.

2 Kate Raworth, "Why Degrowth has Outgrown Its Own Name," *From Poverty to Power*, December 1, 2015. https://oxfamblogs.org/fp2p/why-degrowth-has-out-grown-its-own-name-guest-post-by-kate-raworth/

3 Giorgos Kallis, "You're Wrong, Kate. Degrowth Is a Compelling Word," *From Poverty to Power*, December 2, 2015. https://oxfamblogs.org/fp2p/youre-wrong-kate-degrowth-is-a-compelling-word/

4 Naomi Klein. "How Will Everything Change Under Climate Change? *Guardian*, March 8, 2015. https://www.theguardian.com/environment/2015/mar/08/how-will-everything-change-under-climate-change

5 Naomi Klein, *This Changes Everything: Capitalism vs. The Climate* (New York: Simon & Schuster, 2014).

6 Elizabeth Kolbert, "Can Climate Change Cure Capitalism?" *New York Review of Books*, December 4, 2014. https://www.nybooks.com/articles/2014/12/04/can-climate-change-cure-capitalism/

7 John de Graaf and David E. Batker, *What's the Economy for, Anyway? Why It's Time to Stop Chasing Growth and Start Pursuing Happiness* (New York: Bloomsbury Press, 2012).
8 Tim Jackson, *Prosperity without Growth: The Transition to a Sustainable Economy* (UK Sustainable Development Commission, 2009) http://www.sd-commission.org.uk/data/files/publications/prosperity_without_growth_report.pdf
9 Tim Jackson, *Prosperity Without Growth: Foundations for the Economy of Tomorrow*, 2nd edn. (London: Routledge, 2017). For more background information, see: The Center for the Understanding of Sustainable Prosperity https://www.cusp.ac.uk/themes/aetw/pwg/
10 Jackson, *Prosperity Without Growth*, 2009, ch. 11.
11 Paul Gilding, *The Great Disruption: Why the Climate Crisis Will Bring the End of Shopping and the Birth of a New World* (New York: Bloomsbury, 2011).
12 Institute for Advanced Sustainability Studies https://www.iass-potsdam.de/en; Stockholm Resilience Center https://www.stockholmresilience.org/; Wellbeing Economy Alliance https://wellbeingeconomy.org/; Center for the Advancement of the Steady State Economy https://steadystate.org/; New Economy Coalition https://neweconomy.net/; The Next System Project https://thenextsystem.org/; Sustainable Consumption Research and Action Initiative https://scorai.org/; One Earth https://www.oneearth.org/; Degrow US https://www.degrowus.org/; New Economics Foundation https://neweconomics.org/; Front Porch Republic https://www.frontporchrepublic.com/; Club of Rome https://www.clubofrome.org/; European Economists for an Alternative Economic Policy in Europe http://www.euromemo.eu/about/index.html; Post-Growth Economics Network https://postgrowtheconomics.wordpress.com/; Institute for Future-Fit Economics (ZOE) https://www.facebook.com/pg/zoe.inst/about/; Institute for New Economic Thinking https://www.ineteconomics.org/research/experts/tjackson; Yale Program on Climate Change Communication https://climatecommunication.yale.edu/; Institute for Sustainable Communication http://www.sustainablecommunication.org/; Center for Sustainable Economy https://sustainable-economy.org/who-we-are/; The Balaton Group http://

www.balatongroup.org/; Future Earth https://futureearth.org/

13 Robert Orzanna, "What Europe Needs Is a Sustainability and Wellbeing Pact," *Research and Degrowth*, May 7, 2019. https://degrowth.org/2019/05/07/what-europe-needs-is-a-sustainability-and-wellbeing-pact/

14 Robert J. Shiller, "Narrative Economics," National Bureau of Economic Research, Working Paper 23075, January 2017. https://www.nber.org/papers/w23075.pdf

15 The Story of Stuff Project. https://storyofstuff.org/about/

16 The Story of Stuff Project, "The Story of Solutions." https://storyofstuff.org/movies/the-story-of-solutions/

Index